Nae Expectations

Gary McNair, after Charles Dickens

methuen | drama

LONDON • NEW YORK • OXFORD • NEW DELHI • SYDNEY

METHUEN DRAMA
Bloomsbury Publishing Plc
50 Bedford Square, London, WC1B 3DP, UK
1385 Broadway, New York, NY 10018, USA
29 Earlsfort Terrace, Dublin 2, Ireland

BLOOMSBURY, METHUEN DRAMA and the Methuen
Drama logo are trademarks of Bloomsbury Publishing Plc

First published in Great Britain 2023

Image credit: Joe Connolly/JamHot
Print design: JamHot
Pictured: Gerry Mulgrew as Abel Magwitch
and Karen Dunbar as Miss Havisham

A catalogue record for this book is available from the British Library.

Library of Congress Control Number: 2023947495

ISBN: PB: 978-1-3504-5692-1
ePDF: 978-1-3504-5693-8
eBook: 978-1-3504-5694-5

Series: Modern Plays

Typeset by Mark Heslington Ltd, Scarborough, North Yorkshire

To find out more about our authors and books visit
www.bloomsbury.com and sign up for our newsletters.

Tron Theatre Company presents

Nae Expectations

by Gary McNair after Charles Dickens

Nae Expectations was first performed at Tron Theatre, Glasgow on Thursday 19 October 2023.

ALBA | CHRUTHACHAIL

Nae Expectations
By Gary McNair after Charles Dickens

Joe Gargery/Kelvin Pocket	**Simon Donaldson**
Miss Havisham	**Karen Dunbar**
Mrs Joe/Estella	**Jamie Marie Leary**
Abel Magwitch	**Gerry Mulgrew**
Mr Pumblechook/Jaggers	**Grant Smeaton**
Pip	**Gavin Jon Wright**

All other parts played by The Company

Director	**Andy Arnold**
Dramaturg	**Douglas Maxwell**
Set Design	**Jenny Booth**
Costume Design	**Victoria Brown**
Lighting Design	**Benny Goodman**
Sound Design & Composer	**Ross Brown**
Video Design	**Lewis den Hertog**
Stage Manager	**Suzanne Goldberg**
Deputy Stage Manager	**Kara Jackson**
Assistant Stage Manager	**Jasmine Dittman**
Wardrobe Deputy	**Laura Montgomery**
Production Manager	**Laura Skinner**
Technical Manager	**Mark Hughes**
Technical Stage Manager	**Jason McQuaide**
Venue Technician	**Alex Hatfield**
Set Construction	**Pretty Scenic**

With thanks to: Helen Breen, MUA
Royal Conservatoire of Scotland
Citizens Theatre
Royal Lyceum Theatre
National Theatre of Scotland
Scottish Opera
Bard in the Botanics
Ambassador Theatre Group
Jerry Burns
Jenni Martin
Theatre Gu Leòr
Eoin Carey

ANDY ARNOLD – Director

Andy became Artistic Director of Tron Theatre in 2008 following many years as Artistic Director of The Arches, a venue and theatre company he personally established in 1991. Productions Andy has staged for Tron Theatre Company include: *The Drawer Boy* by Michael Healey; the Scottish premiere of *That Face* by Polly Stenham; *Valhalla* by Paul Rudnick (UK premiere) and world premieres of *Sea and Land and Sky* by Abigail Docherty; *Plume* by J.C. Marshall and *Edwin Morgan's Dreams – And Other Nightmares* by Liz Lochhead.

Most recently, he directed *Cyprus Avenue* by David Ireland, which will be re-mounted at the Pavilion Theatre, Glasgow in early 2024; *La Performance*, a co-production with the International Visual Theatre, Paris and John Byrne's *Underwood Lane* in a co-production with OneRen supported by Future Paisley.

Other directorial work includes his own adaptation of Shakespeare's *The Tempest* with an all-female cast; a promenade show, *high man pen meander* created during lockdown for digital release as a tribute to the work of Edwin Morgan; Gary McNair's adaptation of *The Alchemist*; Enda Walsh's *Ballyturk*; Martin McCormick's *Ma, Pa and the Little Mouths*; Stephen Adly Guirgis' *The Motherfucker with the Hat*; Anthony Neilson's *The Lying Kind*; Martin McDonagh's *The Lonesome West*; Peter Arnott's *Shall Roger Casement Hang?*; Megan Barker's adaptation of Ibsen's *Ghosts*; Samuel Beckett's *Happy Days*, starring Karen Dunbar; a new adaptation by John Byrne of Chekhov's *Three Sisters*; another Byrne work *Colquhoun & MacBryde*; as well as the first stage production of James Joyce's *Ulysses* adapted by Dermot Bolger, which toured to Ireland after its premiere at the Tron. *Ulysses* was revived in 2015 and invited to perform in four cities in China. While in China Andy also staged a devised piece with Chinese actors entitled *A Journey Round James Joyce,* translated into Mandarin and returned to direct *The Selfish Giant* for Beijing Children's Theatre Company. *Nae Expectations* will be Andy's last directorial outing for Tron Theatre Company as he steps down from his role as Artistic Director after almost sixteen years.

JENNY BOOTH – Set Design

Jenny Booth is a set designer and illustrator living and working in Glasgow. Since graduating from the Royal Conservatoire of Scotland in 2017, she has worked extensively for the Tron Theatre, as well as companies such as Citizens Theatre, Solar Bear, Wonder Fools and National Theatre of Scotland. Enjoying a diverse mix of theatre work, she engages in all aspects encompassing set design from scenic art to props and puppet design as well as community outreach roles. Her previous work has included everything from intimate touring productions to entirely recycled main stage shows through which she channels her interest in sustainable theatre.

Recent credits include: *Wake Up* (Solar Bear); *The Bank of Springburn* (National Theatre of Scotland); *Maud's Map* (Citizens Theatre); *The Food of Love*, *Me and My Sister Tell Each Other Everything*, *The Tempest*, *Ali the Magic Elf* (Tron Theatre); *And Then Came the Nightjars* (Wonder Fools).

ROSS BROWN – Sound Design & Composer

Ross graduated from the University of Glasgow with an M.A. in Music and works as a Composer, Musical Director and Sound Designer.

Credits include: *UCI World Cycling Championships*; *The Steamie – OVO Hydro & 30th Anniversary Tour* (Neil Laidlaw); *Generation Dance* (Scottish Ballet/YDance); *Safe To Be Me, Vessel* (Scottish Ballet); *Breath Cycle II* (Scottish Opera); *Submarine Time Machine* and *Tin Forest* (National Theatre of Scotland); *The Steamie, Deathtrap, Witness For The Prosecution* and *And Then There Were None* (Dundee Rep); *A New Life* (Òran Mór/Traverse); *The Wonderful Wizard of Oz, The Dead Letter Detectives, Pushing It, Olive the Other Reindeer, Cinderfella, Trajectories, Mammy Goose, Ma, Pa and the Little Mouths, Chimera, Alice in Weegieland, The Snaw Queen, Sleeping Betty, Ghosts, Miracle on 34 Parnie Street, Three Sisters, A Present State, Ulysses, Aganeza Scrooge* and *Edwin Morgan's Dreams – And Other Nightmares* (Tron Theatre); *Divided City* (Citizens Theatre); *And The Beat Goes On* (Random Accomplice/Perth Theatre); *Our Country's Good* (RCS); *Doras Dùinte* (Theatre Gu Leòr/ Mull Theatre); *Harold & Maude, A Steady Rain* and *Lady M: His Fiend-Like Queen* (Theatre Jezebel); *Clockwork* (Visible Fictions); *In an Alien Landscape, The Man Who Lived Twice* and *Mother Courage* (Birds of Paradise). Other companies Ross has worked with include: Sleeping Warrior, Pavilion Theatre, Scottish Youth Theatre, British Youth Music Theatre, Platform, Impact Arts, MT4UTH-Belfast, OYCI, Glasgow City Council and the BBC.

VICTORIA BROWN – Costume Design

Since graduating from Queen Margaret University, Edinburgh, Victoria has enjoyed being involved in numerous theatre, film and television productions, working with companies including BBC, ITV, Netflix, Discovery Channel, Scottish Opera and Scottish Ballet. Victoria has loved being part of the Tron Theatre creative family since 2015.

SIMON DONALDSON – Joe Gargery / Kelvin Pocket

Simon trained at the Royal Conservatoire of Scotland.

Recent theatre credits include: *Thora* (St Magnus); *Underwood Lane, Ali the Magic Elf* and *Ballyturk* (Tron Theatre); *GHOSTS* (National Theatre of Scotland); *Emergence* (Mull Theatre); *What Girls Are Made Of* (RAW Material/Traverse); *The Strange Undoing of Prudencia Hart* (Eastern Angles); *Variant, When the Penny Drops, Dusty Won't Play, Thoughts Spoken Aloud From Above, Lovesick Blues: The Hank Williams Story, Elf Analysis, Turbo Folk, 200* and *The Ching Room* (Òran Mór); *Hello Dolly, Present Laughter, A Chorus of Disapproval* and *Lady Windemere's Fan* (Pitlochry Festival Theatre); *Tam O'Shanter* and *Zlata's Diary* (Communicado); *The Not So Fatal Death of Grandpa Fredo* (Vox Motus); *The Adventures of Robin Hood, The Spokesman, Jason and the Argonauts, Big Baby* and *The Curse of the Demeter* (Visible Fictions).

Recent radio credits include: *Lamentation, Weir of Hermiston, This Thing of Darkness, For The Love of Leo, Pillow Book, Nest Eggs, Paul Temple, Sullom Voe, McLevy, The Pearl, Rebus, Maigret, The Heart of Midlothian, Dr Korczak's Example, Westway* and *Book at Bedtime.*

Television and film credits include: *Screw, The Lost King, Outlander, Andrew Marr's Great Scots: The Writers Who Shaped a Nation, Outpost 2: Black Sun, Behold Me Standing* and *No More Shall We Part.*

KAREN DUNBAR – Miss Havisham

Karen Dunbar is one of Scotland's best-known entertainers. Starting off in the sketch show *Chewin' the Fat*, she then went on to star in her own show, *The Karen Dunbar Show,* which received 4 Golden Rose nominations.

Karen has trod the boards in every way, from Glasgow pantomime to London's West End, performed Burns, Shakespeare, stand up and DJ-ed, all in New York, and opened the 2014 Commonwealth Games in front of one billion viewers. From community centres to the National Theatre, Karen has captivated audiences with her mix of comedy, music and her acting talents. She recently headlined in the national tour of *Calendar Girls: The Musical* and played Lady Bracknell in *The Importance of Being Earnest* at Perth Rep.

Karen's BBC Scotland documentary #CancelKarenDunbar has gathered much interest and been an important talking point amongst many Scots. In her new BBC Scotland documentary, *Karen Dunbar's School of Rap*, Karen and five older women go on a hip-hop journey from page to stage. Both documentaries can be viewed on BBC iPlayer.

BENNY GOODMAN – Lighting Design

Benny Goodman is a freelance lighting designer and creative collaborator, based in Glasgow and London.

He has worked in theatres across the UK and Europe on a variety of projects and productions, and is a creative collaborator with theatre company, Wonder Fools.

Selected credits include: *4 Walls* and *The Palace of Varieties* (Derby Theatre); *La Performance* (Tron Theatre/IVT Paris); *A Midsummer Night's Dream* (Orange Tree Theatre); *Hamlet* (Saint Stephen's Theatre); *hang, The Tempest* and *The Mistress Contract* (Tron Theatre); *Sense of Centre* (Dance Base); *Julius Caesar* (Company of Wolves/Scottish tour); *Learning from the Future* (OGR Torino); *Meet Jan Black* (Ayr Gaiety); *Maim and Heroines* (Theatre Gu Leòr); *I Can Go Anywhere* (Traverse Theatre); *The Drift* (National Theatre of Scotland); *The Afflicted* (Summerhall); *Country Music* (Omnibus Theatre); *549: Scots of the Spanish Civil War* (Wonder Fools/UK tour); *Daddy Drag* (Assembly Roxy); *Where We Are: The Mosque* (Arcola Theatre, London); *Sorella Mia* (The Place, London); *Disarming Reverberations* (St Giles Cathedral, Edinburgh); *Humbug* (Tramway, Glasgow); *Snow Queen* (Associate – Dundee Rep Theatre); *Like Animals* (SUPERFAN); *Ayanfe Opera* (Bridewell Theatre, London); *Lampedusa* (Citizens Theatre) and *Circle of Fifths* (Royal Conservatoire of Scotland/Cockpit Theatre, London).

For more on his work – www.bennygoodman.co

JAMIE MARIE LEARY – Mrs Joe / Estella

Jamie is a Bajan/Scottish actress who trained at Langside College in the south side of Glasgow. Since graduating in 2014, Jamie has worked regularly in Scottish theatre. However, for the past few years she has been adding to a growing list of television credits including appearances in BBC One comedy drama *Ralph & Katie* and in *River City*.

Theatre credits include: *Anna Karenina* (Royal Lyceum/Bristol Old Vic); *Expensive Sh*t* (Soho Theatre/Traverse Theatre); *The Celtic Story* (Bublico Productions); *Class Act: Silver* and *Breakfast Plays: B!RTH* (Traverse Theatre); *Locker Room Talk* (Traverse Theatre/Latitude Festival); *Stand By* (Utter Theatre/Byre Theatre); *549: Scots of the Spanish Civil War* (Wonder Fools); *Cinderella* and *A Christmas Carol* (Citizens Theatre); and *Holding/Holding On* (National Theatre of Scotland).

Television credits include: *Ralph & Katie, River City, Casualty* and *The Nest* (BBC); and *Traces* (Alibi/BBC).

Film credits include: *Hen-Do* (BFI); *Car Sick* (Particular Films); *Shepherd* (GC Films); *Super November* (14c Studios); and *Where Do We Go From Here* (Worrying Drake).

GARY McNAIR – Writer

Gary McNair is a writer and performer from Glasgow who aims to entertain and challenge audiences in equal measure. His work has been translated into several languages and performed in America, Australia, Italy, Germany, Russia, Portugal, New Zealand, Brazil, Turkey and Japan. He is a mainstay of the Edinburgh Fringe where his last seven shows have sold out and he has won the coveted Scotsman Fringe First Award three times. He is Writer in Residence at the National Theatre of Scotland and an Associate Artist at the Traverse Theatre in Edinburgh and at the Tron. He loves telling stories and is delighted that people want to hear them.

Recent works include: *Dear Billy* (National Theatre of Scotland); *Jekyll and Hyde* (Reading Rep/Royal Lyceum Theatre); *Black Diamonds and the Blue Brazil* (Royal Lyceum Theatre); *The Alchemist* (Tron Theatre); *Square Go* (co-authored by Kieran Hurley) (Francesca Moody Productions/Paines Plough); *McGonagall's Chronicles* (Òran Mòr); *Locker Room Talk/Letters to Morrissey* (Traverse Theatre); *A Gambler's*

Guide To Dying (Show and Tell/Traverse Theatre). Many of these titles and more are available from www.bloomsbury.com

GERRY MULGREW – Abel Magwitch

After obtaining an MA in French and Philosophy from the University of Glasgow, Gerry Mulgrew worked in childrens' and community theatre before founding the theatre company Communicado in 1983, becoming its artistic director in 1986. His directing credits for Communicado include: Edwin Morgan's translation of *Cyrano de Bergerac* (commissioned by the company), *The Cone Gatherers*; the world premiere of *Mary Queen of Scots Got Her Head Chopped Off*; *Jock Tamson's Bairns, Blood Wedding, The Suicide*; Gogol's *The Government Inspector* and his own adaptation of *Tam O' Shanter*.

His notable recent acting credits include: *River City* (BBC); *The Silver Superheroes* and *Losing the Rag* (Òran Mór); *Ma, Pa and the Little Mouths*, *high man pen meander* and *Krapp's Last Tape* (Tron Theatre); *Still* (Traverse Theatre); *Lanark: A Life in Three Acts* (Citizens Theatre/ EIF); *The Tree of Knowledge* (Traverse Theatre); *Scenes for Survival: The Maid's Room* (National Theatre of Scotland); *Lost at Sea* (Perth Theatre); Old Peer in *Peer Gynt* (National Theatre of Scotland/Dundee Rep) for which he won a joint CATS Award for Best Male Performance; Vladimir in *Waiting for Godot* (Citizens Theatre); and Folly in *Ane Pleasant Satyre of the Thrie Estaitis* with Edinburgh University.

Gerry has also directed for numerous other companies including the Royal Shakespeare Company (*Moby Dick*) and recently with the Xinchan Company in Beijing, China where he mounted a series of Beckett shorts in Mandarin. Throughout his career he had received a number of awards including six Fringe Firsts for Outstanding New Work at the Edinburgh Festival, three Edinburgh Evening News Awards, the Edinburgh Festival Hamada Prize, a Herald Angel Award and the Inaugural Prudential Award for British Theatre.

GRANT SMEATON – Mr Pumblechook / Jaggers

Grant Smeaton was born and lives in Glasgow. He was part of Andy Arnold's original Arches Theatre team, appearing in *Noise & Smokey Breath, The Devils, Waiting for Godot, Spend a Penny* and many, many more.

He was the founder and has been artistic director of both Hopscotch Theatre Company and Tangerine Productions, directing more than 50 shows for the two companies including *Abigail's Party, Spurt!* and *Torch Song Trilogy*. Work for Glasgay! included productions of *Talking Heads, Kiss of the Spiderwoman* and *Ch Ch Changes*. Grant won a Herald Angel Award for *Bette/Cavett.*

He has appeared in a number of Tron Theatre Company productions including *Valhalla, Bliss+Mud, Monaciello* for the Naples Theatre Festival and *Ulysses*. He has also appeared in productions for, amongst others, Suspect Culture and National Theatre of Scotland, 7:84, X Factor Dance Company and Òran Mór.

Television credits include *Scotch & Wry, Taggart, The Ferguson Theory, Rab C Nesbitt* and *Only An Excuse.*

GAVIN JON WRIGHT – Pip

This is Gavin's fifth main stage production with Tron Theatre Company having previously been involved in *Scenes Unseen, Miracle on 34 Parnie Street, Ulysses* and *The Lying Kind.*

Other theatre credits include work for National Theatre of Scotland, Vox Motus, Glasgow Life, Citizens Theatre, Cumbernauld Theatre, Perth Theatre, Royal Lyceum/Double M Arts, Macrobert, Red Bridge Arts, Ayr Gaiety, Pitlochry Festival Theatre, Grid Iron, Grid Iron/Traverse Theatre, Traverse Theatre/59 East 59 NYC, Random Accomplice, Francesca Moody Productions as well as a number of shows for Òran Mór's A Play, A Pie and A Pint.

Television work includes: *In Plain Sight, Taggart, Still Game, Shetland, Lip Service, Annika, Unfair* and *Dear Green Place.*

Radio and voiceover experience includes work for BBC Radio Drama, Borgen and Ridley Jones.

ABOUT TRON THEATRE

Tron Theatre is a unique and flagship organisation as the West of Scotland's only mid-scale producing venue which delivers challenging new and contemporary performance for the people of Glasgow, Scotland, and worldwide while at the same time playing a vital role at the heart of the Scottish theatre community and facilitating participation in the arts amongst people of all ages, race, ability, and gender.

Recent Tron Theatre Company productions include David Ireland's *Cyprus Avenue*, *La Performance*, a co-production with the International Visual Theatre, Paris, John Byrne's *Underwood Lane*, Eilidh Loan's *Moorcroft*, Gary McNair's adaptation of the Ben Jonson farce, *The Alchemist, The Ugly One* by Marius von Mayenberg, Jo Clifford's adaptation of *The Taming of the Shrew*, Enda Walsh's *Ballyturk*, *Ma, Pa and the Little Mouths* by Martin McCormick, Peter Arnott's *Shall Roger Casement Hang?*, Martin McDonagh's *The Lonesome West* and Isobel McArthur's *Pride and Prejudice* *(*sort of)* – Tron's co-production with Blood of the Young which had its premiere at the venue in 2018, toured nationally, and opened in the autumn of 2021 at the Criterion Theatre in London's West End, receiving an Olivier Award in 2022 for Best Entertainment or Comedy.

Tron Theatre Company is a supported by Creative Scotland and is a Scottish Registered Charity No: SC012081.

If you would like to make a donation to support the work of Tron Theatre please visit, https://www.tron.co.uk/donate/

www.tron.co.uk

Director's Note

I was shocked to discover that this will be the 40th Tron production I've directed. Since I started in 2008, I have always felt immensely privileged to be the keeper of the artistic keys in this glorious Glasgow theatre. I have very few regrets in my choices of plays and have tried to avoid building too many advance expectations as to their outcomes – so this seems a fitting title to be departing on.

Gary McNair and I had great fun collaborating on his adaptation of *The Alchemist* in 2019 and I was delighted with his suggestion for this new venture. The writing in Dickens' original novel is a wonderful mix of dry and caustic wit combined with dark and tragic events – and a story depicting a host of often extraordinary and weird characters. As our title suggests, the action has been shifted to Glasgow and what better place for the portrayal of eccentricity, dastardly deeds, and mayhem? At the heart of the story of course is the emotional and moral deterioration of someone in their pursuit of wealth and social advancement – a journey as familiar now as it ever was.

As with so many previous Tron productions, I am lucky to be joined on this show by such a talented group of actors and artistic team – some of whom I have worked with during the past three decades and others I have only got to know in very recent years or, indeed, for the first time.

No Tron theatre production could be realised without the commitment of all our dedicated Tron staff – full time, part time, and freelance – working tirelessly behind the scenes and contributing so vitally to the Tron theatre experience … to all of them I will be eternally grateful.

Andy Arnold

Writer's Note

What can I say? This show has been a dream of mine for a long time, but in truth it was for most of that time, a quiet dream, which I held to myself.

You see, there was a time where I thought I would never be able to read Dickens, let alone adapt it for the stage.

I always struggled with reading. I could never keep my attention on a book for long enough to feel like I was following the story. My mind would wander off and I would end up rereading sections over and over again. The idea of reading for pleasure, of devouring great works always struck me as a very aspirational quality, a quality I'd often feel quietly ashamed that I didn't possess. Very occasionally, a writer's voice would chime with me and I would devour a book and I would immediately declare to myself that 'this is it, I've cracked it! If anyone needs me I'll be in the living room ... reading!' But then of course I'd pick up the next book, struggle all over again and I'd be left feeling stupid.

As you can imagine, this led to me feeling intimidated by most literature but especially by the great classics.

I would occasionally pluck up the courage and pick up a classic book and start reading it like an act of combat, more like I was trying to prove it wrong than to glean any pleasure from its pages. But I'd always end up running out of steam very early on, and it would compound the idea these great works would just never be for me.

But then I read a little passage of *Great Expectations*, and it was completely different. It really grabbed me. It was fun. It was exciting. It didn't feel like work at all.

Now, I didn't go on to instantly devour it. Far from it. It took me years to read it, a little bit at a time. It was a great way to do it. It allowed me to see these classic books less like mountains to be conquered and more as worlds to wander through. And it never become a chore. By the time I'd finished, rather than feel embarrassed about how long it took me, I felt like I'd had the luxury of spending a long time with these characters and had the chance to really fall in love with them. Of course Pip was central to this, I loved his curiosity, I loved his charm, which was far cheekier than any of the depictions I'd seen in any adaptations, and I loved how funny he was. It turns out Dickens is like, genuinely very funny. Who knew? And although I related to very few of the actual situations Pip finds himself in, I related a great deal to a lad who spends his whole life in his head trying to work out what the hell is going on around him and how on earth he plays his part in it.

The whole thing read more like a great big monologue than a novel. It was engaging, direct and like it was begging to spoken aloud.

I knew very early on that I would love to present a version of it one day. I wanted to share the Pip that I saw in the book with the world, with a gallus sense of humour and a big heart.

But how? I'm not the guy that adapts classic books. I should leave that to the people who adapt classics. Surely.

Then in steps Andy Arnold. I'd just performed my rhyming play about William McGonagall at the Tron and he decided to take a punt and ask me if I would like to adapt The Alchemist by Ben Johnson and I'm so glad he did. I said yes straight away, even though (as you can imagine with my relationship to old texts described above) it was a daunting task. But Andy made the whole thing extremely fun and treated me like I knew what I was doing and we had a great time making it. I knew then he'd be the person to ask to direct *Nae Expectations* and I was thrilled that he said yes.

I'm so grateful for the chance to present this show and to Andy and the Tron having faith in me to do it and for assembling such a wonderful cast and creative team. The fact that it is going to be Andy's 40th and final production here at the Tron is a particular honour.

I hope you enjoy reading/watching it as much as we did making it.

Gary

Nae Expectations

For Katy, Rosa and Leo

List of characters

Pip
Abel Magwitch (Convict)
Mrs Joe
Joe Gargery
Mrs Hubble
Uncle Pumblechook
Sgt McLunstry
Estella
Miss Havisham
Kelvin Pocket
Busker
Jaggers
Bar Staff
Driver
Martha
Man in Street
Officer

There are other parts which are listed in the script – mainly voices.

A solidus / indicates an interruption.

Act One

Scene One

Music stirs as we start to see through the downstage gauze.

A man enters a dim lit forge.

He is wearing a top hat and a long coat.

He looks around the place taking it all in.

It's very familiar. But it is strange to be back here.

He takes off his hat and sets it down.

The gauze rises.

He takes off his jacket.

He sees there is a slight ember in the fire.

He pokes his cane in the ashes.

He rolls his sleeves up.

He pokes at it again.

Pip (*to audience*)   OK. How do I?

Where do I?

How do I even start? It's a mental story. Ah know, Ah know, everyone says that – ma life's pure mental. But honestly – a guy nearly drowns, a man eats a live pigeon (though Ah might no have time for that), A WOMAN GETS SET ON FIRE – RIGHT BEFORE MY EYES!

But before we get tae aw that, Ah should tell you ma name. Right. So . . . ma name, is . . . Pip. But it isny. Right, so ma da's name, well no just his, but like the family name is . . . Pirrip. Right?

Which is . . . aye.

And Ah know yer thinkin' 'Ye canna have a name lit Pirrip, that's no a real name!'

He walks across to grave stones . . . mist starts to roll across floor.

But Ah do and it is. And Ah know 'cause I read it on ma dad's tombstone. And ma mum's. And aw ma brothers and sisters that didny make it. 'Cause they're aw, hingy, you know . . . deed. Which is why they've got the tombstone. Obviously.

So Pirrip.

Right.

Which, on its own is no that fuckin . . . it's no your Hubble's, yer Magwitch's, yer Pumblechooks.

Right, but see if you team it up wi the right first name it can really, ye know.

And ma first name is . . . Phillip.

Phillip. Pirrip.

Aye. That's *ma* name.

And here, right, see when Ah was wee, right, like when Ah was really wee, Ah couldn'y say it.

Ah tried!

But Ah couldn'y get ma tongue round aw the maddeningly subtle differences of this ridiculously similar first and second name.

So, you'd think folk would be like:

Maw's Grave (*V/O*)   Oh my god, that's amazing. Our baby, our wonderful baby, who's not even one year old yet, I might add, is trying to say his name.

Da's Grave (*V/O*)   That is remarkable. Now, it's not quite there. But heavens alive it's a hell of an effort given that it is a very difficult name to say, and what with him having barely entered the holophrastic stage of speech development and so his brain must be wise beyond the current physical limits of his tongues dexterity.

Maw's Grave   What a bright one we have here!

Da's Grave   Such potential.

Maw's Grave   Let's do all we can to encourage him. Who knows what he might achieve. Look out world. Here he comes.

Pip   But naw, they were just like

Da's Grave   Ha, that stupit fuckin baby cannae talk! Hinks his name's Pip!

Maw's Grave   Haaa, idiot. Let's call him Pip. Forever.

Pip (*to audience*)   So, aye, that's erm, that's how Ah came to get ma name.

And Ah guess that maybe geez ye a wee bit eh an insight intae. You know, what's goin on up (*Points to head.*) there. Goes in deep that stuff.

Can fair fuck ye up.

Ah'm no saying lit that man. Pure – Ah'm pure fucked up, man.

Naw, Ah'm no bragging like that.

Some folk roon here can pure brag about that stuff. Pure.

A guy stoats into shot – staggering. Bottle in brown paper bag.

Random One   Aw here, see me, Ah'm pure fucked up by the way, so fuckin watch it.

Pip (*to audience*)   Naw, no like that, that's no me.

So, who am Ah then?

Well . . .

OK . . .

He takes in his surroundings

. . . we'll start here.

Graveyard

I'm seven years old and I'm out past the marshes at my parents' graves.

Ah come here and talk tae them a lot.

Is that no sad?

See if I met a guy and he told me what ha've just told you?

Man . . . I'd be like that.

Right?

Random One (*going offstage*)   Sad bastard.

Pip (*to audience*)   But that's how it wis.

I know it might sound daft. Like, I'd be as well talking tae a stream or a lake or a fence post. But, like, I feel . . . connected to them. Here. Even if they did give me a stupit fuckin name like Phillip Pirrip.

So I'm sat here one day in the peace and quiet, havin' a bit eh a chat wi them, lit, ye know 'Is this aw there is? Am Ah ever gonnae come tae anyhin'? Is this really aw there is?' Ye know, aw that stuff, and havin' a bit of a cry, probably when suddenly . . . there's a hushed and violent bark of:

Voice   You! Shut your fucking mouth!

Pip (*to audience*)   Now, as a generally terrified wee boy Ah thought Ah'd shat masel loads.

A man emerges and heads **Pip**'s *way.*

But it was only now, that I could *truly* consider myself shat.

The man has now traversed the stage and towers over **Pip** *who is trembling.*

Pip   I'm, I'm, I'm sorry. Please don't hurt me.

Convict   I said SHUT YOUR FUCKIN MOUTH.

Pip   I'm sorry, I don't mean to, I'm just /

Convict   / Make another noise and rip your fuckin lungs out and boot them clean across that field like a rugby ball. D'ye understand?!

Terrified and silent, **Pip** *nods.*

The **Convict** *scans the perimeter for danger like a silverback, always keeping half an eye on* **Pip***, formulating a plan as to how he can use this boy to his advantage.*

Convict   What's yer name?

Pip   . . .

Convict   You no hear me?! I said *WHAT'S YER NAME?!*

Pip   Sorry. Sorry. I just . . . you said to shut it. And and and . . . my lungs. I just

Convict   NAME!

Pip   I'm sorry. I'm just scared . . . I'm scared. It's Pip.

Convict   It's what? Speak up, man.

Pip   Pip. My names Pip. My name's Pip!

Convict   Right. Where you live, Pip?

Pip   . . . Erm . . . just over

Convict   Where?!

Pip   There. Right over there. With the lights! You see the lights? There!

Convict   Right. You got any wittles on you?

Pip   Well I . . . I don't know!

Convict   Oh for god's sake, just . . . fuckin . . .

The **Convict** *grabs* **Pip** *and turns him upside down and shakes him. Nothing but a piece of bread falls out of him.*

The **Convict** *grabs the bread and devours it like an animal before turning his attention to* **Pip** *who is sat on a tombstone.*

Convict   You nothing else?

Pip   No. Sorry. Nothin' / I

Convict   / You've got fat wee cheeks. How'd you get fat wee cheeks wi nuhin but a wee dod eh bread tae eat?! . . . I've got half a mind tae rip them aff and eat them.

Pip   Please . . . don't?

Convict   Shut it. Where's yer maw.

Pip   There.

Convict   Fuck!

He takes a short run for cover before realising he can't see anyone.

Convict   Fuck you talking about? Where?!

Pip   There, sir.

Maw's Grave (*V/O*)   I'm here, ya daft bastart!

Pip *points at the tombstone.*

Pip   That's her, 'Al . . . Al . . . Also Georgiana'.

Convict   Oh. Right. Eh . . . Is that yer da there n'all?

Pip   Ye . . . yeah . . . Yes. 'Late of this Parish'.

Convict   Right. OK. Who do you live with then?

That's if Ah let ye live. Ah've no decided that yet!

Pip   Ah live with ma sister! . . . Mrs Gargery, and Mr Joe! Joe! Joe Gargery, the blacksmith.

Convict   Blacksmith?

He glances at his ankle and back at **Pip**.

Convict Blacksmith?!

Back at the ankle, back at **Pip**.

Convict Fuckin blacksmith?!

Delighted, he starts pacing. Excited.

Pip Yeah, it's . . . they make things from wrought iron and steel.

Convict I know what a fuckin' blacksmith is ya . . . right, quiet a minute.

Just. OK. OK, you might just have bought your survival.

Now, listen up and you listen up, good!

He leans in close, so close to **Pip** *that he sprays bits of bread into his face.*

Convict You know what a file is?

Pip Yes!

Convict Right. And you know what wittles is?

Pip . . . Eh . . .

Convict Christ alive! It's food. Wittles is food!

Pip OK. Sorry.

Convict You bring me a file and you bring me wittles!

He has now tilted **Pip** *so far back he is horizontal.*

Convict You bring them both to me.

Another tilt down, beyond horizontal. **Pip** *looks like he'll be sick.*

Convict OK?!

He drags **Pip** *right back to meet his gaze.*

Convict Because without them I'm dead. And if I'm dead, it'll be your fault I'm dead. And I'll tell you this – I'll no take kindly to being dead. And I'll take even less kindly to the poor bastart that's killed me. OK?

Pip   Yes.

Convict   Good. Now, I am gonna make a couple of things perfectly clear before you go. If I die tonight, I'll make it my mission in the after life to find these two (*Points at mum and dad's grave.*) and batter them!

Before coming back here to find and haunt the living piss out of you.

And if the after life doesn't scare you.

Know this . . . I'm not alone.

There's someone else out here.

Under me command.

Someone far scarier than me.

Someone who makes me look like a fuckin saint.

He is hungry and he has his mind set on you.

But! When you deliver what I need.

And ONLY when you deliver what I need will I call him off.

And if you don't.

That man,

That monster,

Who is listening and watching right now.

And who knows your face.

That monster that has special and peculiar ways of getting at a boy's heart and liver.

Ways that never ever fail.

He will get you.

You can lock your door.

Hide in bed.

Or run away.

Run for miles.

Run for weeks and months and years.

But he will get you.

Do you understand?

Pip   Yes sir.

Convict   Right. Now go now and god help you if you come across my friend on your way 'cause he'll no give you a chance like Ah huv. Now go. GO!

Pip (*to audience*)   Ah ran like fuck over the marshes and didn't glance back until I was sure Ah'd covered enough ground so that he'd maybe eh stopped watching me run.

Then I remember his cannibal friend, shit myself anew and run all the way home.

Back Home

Now, you'd think in a scenario like this that I'd feel some sort of relief from getting back to the house. You'd *think* I'd feel safe from having reached the sanctuary of home.

You would think that. But that's because you've never lived wi ma sister.

And Ah don't mean tae speak bad eh anyone, right, and I know everyone says Ah should be grateful 'cause she stepped in and 'raised me by hand' but the thing wi ma sister, right, is that she's eh. Well, she's a wee bit . . . demonic.

We see **Mrs Joe**'s *face looking demonic.*

Pip (*to audience*)   So, as I enter, I am as on edge as ever. Then Joe goes:

Joe   Psssst. Pip! Pssst Quick. In here!

Pip *enters.* **Joe** *is happy to see him but is very much keeping an edge out for* **Pip**'s *sister.*

Joe   Listen Pip, it's good tae see ye lad but Mrs Joe's looking for you. She's absolutely bealin'. She's been out twelve times awreddy and that's her out again makin' it a baker's dozen. She's purple-heptic so she is. On the absolute rampage. And Pip . . . she's got tickler with her.

Pip   Bastart!

(*To audience.*) Tickler is a stick. Her favourite stick. And her main support in raising me 'by hand'.

Joe   Quick, Pip, hide!

Mrs Joe *bursts in.*

Pip   Ah!!!

Mrs Joe   Where is that little shit?!

Joe *covers* **Pip** *as he makes a dash to hide behind the door.*

Mrs Joe   I swear to god if he's gone and got himself killed this time there's nuhin you could blame me for. If it wasn't for me pushing meals inside him like a lame duck he'd've been eaten by wolves or pigs or fuckin . . . kittens years ago!

Joe (*sheepishly*)   Now, come on, he's an alright lad I supp / ose

Mrs Joe   / You what?! Am I gonna have to use this on you ya

She raises the tickler over her head. **Pip** *jumps out to take the attention off* **Joe**.

Pip   Sorry Ah'm late, Ah was just, eh.

Mrs Joe   Just what?! What the fuck have you been doing? And where the fuck have you been?!

Pip   Sorry I was, eh, I was just up at the graveyard.

Mrs Joe Graveyard? Graveyard?! I'll give you bloody graveyard! If it wasn't for me raisin you by hand you'd have been put there permanently. Years ago!

And Ah tell you, it's some bloody miracle that I have managed it. I have lived three lives caring for you, boy, and none of them fun.

When I do finally shuffle off this mortal coil I should get to spend eternity as a saint, as a fucking saint, you hear me?! But knowing ma luck I'll come back as a bloody gnat or a newt or a dung beetle or some other poor wretched soul that works too hard and dies too young.

Pip Ah was just seeing Mum and Dad.

Mrs Joe Well they ain't coming back, now come here!

She readies tickler for a strike.

Pip (*to audience*) And Ah don't know where it comes from, maybe because I'd just survived the man out on the marshes, but Ah say . . .

(*To* **Mrs Joe.**) . . . no?

Mrs Joe Oh, so it's like that, is it?

She makes a lunge for him and he very nimbly moves, she is dumbfounded, **Pip***, maybe more so, he's committed now, she lunges again, and again he dodges, two, three more lunges, but . . . he's taken one step too many, backed into a corner, she has him now, they both know it.*

Mrs Joe Who raised you by hand? Eh? Who (*Whack.*). Raised (*Whack.*). You (*Whack.*). By (*Whack.*). Hand? (*Whack.*).

Pip You.

Mrs Joe Who?!

Pip You!!!

Mrs Joe That's right! I did! And don't you ever forget it!

She now sets about whacking him relentlessly. It is joyless, thorough and so routine that it is very hard to watch.

Mrs Joe   Right. Dinner! Honestly, what the hell would you two do without me?

Pip *and* **Joe** *share a brief, hopeful look at each other to dream of what that might be like, but it mustn't last long for she could catch them and they can't afford such fantasies.*

Mrs Joe *grabs the bread. She butters it, halves it and dishes it out with a somewhat violent precision. It is a paltry offering.*

Mrs Joe   Right. Get this ett.

The slamming down of the bread has brought about a nervous silence and thus begins a physical routine. As soon as **Mrs Joe** *is out of sight,* **Joe** *picks up his bread with giddy excitement. Not because he can't wait to eat it but because he gets to play with it. He starts making the bread dance . . .* **Joe** *is a little surprised and gutted to see* **Pip** *is just staring at his food, as paltry an amount as it is, with longing and hungry eyes.*

The **Convict** *appears. He is only here in* **Pip**'s *mind.*

Convict   Are you seriously thinking about fucking eating that?

When that might be the only food you can get your hands on.

Go on then, eat it. It'll be your last fuckin meal if you do!

Joe *is crestfallen that he can't get* **Pip** *to engage so he takes a sad bite of his bread. His sadness doesn't last long though because he's struck with the wonderful idea of biting his bread into a shape, maybe a boat? Or a gun? That'll amuse* **Pip**. *Still nothing. He slumps his shoulders and takes an even sadder bite.*

Convict   Seriously, if he even touches ma bread I'm gonna get him eaten anaw!

Pip *takes this opportunity, with* **Joe** *looking glumly at the floor, to snaffle his entire piece of bread down his trouser leg. Gone quick as a flash.*

Convict   That's it. Good lad. Fuckin gooood lad.

Joe, *unaware of any activity, takes a brief glance up at* **Pip** *and then a double take. He is in excited disbelief.*

Mrs Joe *clocks something's wrong.*

Mrs Joe   Fuck's the matter wi you pair?!

Convict   Shut her up. And keep her away fae ma bread. Tell her ye farted or something.

Pip   Eh . . . nothing, Ah just farted! But don't worry it, dunt stink but so all good.

She skelps **Pip** *and wanders off.*

Mrs Joe   Filthy begger!

Joe   Seriously but, Pip, you canna be dayin that.

Pip   Dayin what? I'm no doin nuthin man, fuck up.

Joe   Nah man, it's serious, ye canna be hoofin' yer food lit that, man.

Need tae chew it, man.

It's like it's no even . . . been in yer mooth at all!

Convict   Fuckin shut this guy up.

Pip   Seriously man, wheesht!

Joe   Ah will. But Ah'll say this before Ah do.

Hoofin yer food like that might feel fun.

But your storin' problems for yersel man.

Seriously, that kind eh hoofin could kill a boy,

Christ man, hoofin like that could kill a horse!

Pip   Right ye are, Joe, yer a good lad, Joe, thanks, I'll take more care next time.

Joe   Right. Good lad, Pip.

Convict   Aye, good lad. But you're gonna need to bring me more than that!

The **Convict** *drifts away.*

Re-enter **Mrs Joe***.*

Mrs Joe   OK, whatever shite you two are spewin', shut it, and come here and get yer /

Pip   Dontsaytarwaterdontsaytarwaterdontsaytarwater

Mrs Joe   / tarwater

Pip   Bastart!

Mrs Joe   Ye whit?! I didn't raise you by hand so you ye could talk like that!

Now c'mere and get tarred, ya bastart!

Trust you tae no know whit's good fir you!

Pip (*to audience*)   Now, Ah can't really describe to you how brutal this supposed medicine was. Imagine, right, if a train could take a piss . . . that.

Mrs Joe *grabs his face, squeezes his lips open and pours in the mixture.*

She loves it.

Pip *staggers in agony having consumed the mixture.*

Joe *is reading in his chair. He cheers in delight!*

Joe   Wow, hell of a book this is, Pip.

Look! There a J. And an O! Joe!

Oh and look, there another J!

Pip   You ever think about learning to read the rest of it, Joe?

Or I could read it to you of you like?

Joe   Oh, I don't know what the rest of it is gonna offer me that could be better than that. One. Two. Five J's and . . . ooft, even more Os than I can count. This is amazin'! Best thing I've read since Jaberwocky. You should see the amount of J, O, Joes in that!

There is an almighty bang outside!

Pip   Was that great guns, Joe?

Joe   Aye, there's another convict off!

Pip   Right . . . Sorry, what does that mean?

Mrs Joe (*cutting in*)   Bloody hell. Escaped. Means they've escaped, ya numpty.

Pip   OK thanks. Sorry . . . who's escaped?

Mrs Joe   See, that's the problem wi this boy. You answer one question and yer hit wi a dozen more. The bloody convicts!

Pip   OK. Gotcha. And . . . sorry, what's a convict?

Joe   Folk that's kept in the hulks.

Pip   Right you are.

Joe   See, he's not so daft.

Pip   And . . . I'm so sorry but . . . What's the hulks?

Mrs Joe   'Not so daft'? Thick as pig shit and half as useful!

Hulks is prison ships.

Pip   Thanks.

Here. Can Ah ask something?

Mrs Joe   Fuck me, now he checks if he can ask something!

Ask no questions, you'll be told no lies!

Pip   Why would you lie?

Mrs Joe   See you ya . . .! Ah didny bring you up by hand so you could badger people's lives away wi endless questions, did Ah?

Pip   No. Yes. OK. Sorry for that. But, like . . . Can Ah ask . . .

So . . . like, why do people end up on the prison ships?

Mrs Joe   Oh, I'll tell you alright . . . they're put there for robbin' and murderdin' and pillagein' an' all manners eh worse. And it all starts . . . wi askin' . . . questions! So huv ye anyhin' else tae ask?!

Ah didn't bloody think so.

Pip   Well, eh . . . Goodnight, I suppose.

Mrs Joe   Eh . . . 'Scuse me!

As much as I'd love you oot ma sight, you've got a Christmas pudding to mix!

Pip (*to audience*)   Oh aye. It's Christmas, by the way! Did I no mention? That might now help you make sense of all the jolly cheer and merriment.

Pip *is given a spoon and is beaten about the head as a means of supervision.*

Mrs Joe   Not steady enough. (*Whack.*)

Stir to the edges as well, not just the middle! (*Whack.*)

You're splashing it out the pot! (*Whack.*)

Pip *gets lost in the stirring. The* **Convict** *reappears.*

Pip *tries to stir harder in the hope that he'll go away.*

Convict   Here. This smells good. You gonna bring me this?

You're no just gonna bring that wee bit eh bread down your leg are ye?

Try and ignore me all you want. I am in there . . . rent free.

What's wrong? You don't want tae rob yer sister?

Her? The way she treats you?! Like a rat in the lavvy?

My god.

I tell ye whit, feed me her.

Put an end tae all our problems.

Pip   Fuck it. What if Ah just say no.

What, you'll eat me? So fuck.

Ah'd rather you just ate me than have tae live wi the guilt eh robbin them.

She's geed me everything Ah've got. Which, as close to fuck all as it is, I'm alive and that's no nuhin'.

Convict   Listen to yourself. Have you any idea what it would be like to eaten alive.

You any idea how long it would take for you to die?

Think it might be worse than a wee bit of shame.

Fuckin idiot.

And here's the thing.

Not robbin' them aint gonna save ye from hell.

Yer already goin tae hell for stealing that bread and lyin' about it.

So you may as well bring me the lot.

And then at least you might live a wee bit longer before you have to go to hell.

Pip   Oh god I'm sorry.

I'm sorry Mrs Joe I'm sorry Mrs Joe I'm sorry Mrs Joe.

Pip *runs off to his room.*

(*To audience.*) Ah don't sleep a wink.

If Ah close my eyes in the slightest it's:

There is a quick transformation to a nightmare . . . menacing soundscape.

Voice overs.

Officer   There he is! There's the boy that's gonna rob his own house.

Get him to the hulks!

Mrs Joe   And me raising him by hand too!

Convict   Me and ma pal are hungry, Pip.

Maw *and* **Da Graves**   How could he let us down like this?

We're literally spinning in our graves!

The gravestones spin around, somehow.

Officer   Look, he's trying to escape!

Catch him. And

Omnes   HANG THE BASTARD

Convict   Hang the bastard? Cook the bastard!

The dream snaps to an end.

Pip   No. NO. NO!!!

Pip *comes to and realises he is in his room.*

(*To audience.*) Fuck that. Sleep can whistle!

So at the very first crack of light, I'm away like a sprinter in the traps!

But like a really quiet, nervous one.

I tell you what, every board, every single one eh them, boards that had never even creaked in their life, are suddenly squeakin' and creakin' and howling and hollerin' as if every wan eh them was goin'

Floorboard (*V/O*)   Mrs Joe, Mrs Joe, wake up Mrs Joe! There a thief oot here! Get out here and boot his baws!

Pip (*to the audience*)   But Ah make it tae the pantry.

Pip *stops just outside the door to gather himself. Takes a deep breath and heads in. The light catches off a pig with an apple in its mouth, It snaps to life:*

Pig   Ah see you ya sneaky bastart.

Pip   I'm sorry, I don't wan't to . . . please don't tell!

The lights snap again and the pig is as dead as disco.

Pip *looks around, he's amazed at how well stocked it is.*

Pip   My god Ah'm hungry. Shut up, Pip. Just grab what you can and run like fuck.

Worry abut eatin' later!

He grabs some bread, a rind of cheese and about half a jar of mincemeat and wraps up in a hanky with last night's slice.

Then he pours some brandy from the stone bottle into a wee glass bottle.

Then he tops up the brandy with liquid from a big jug nearby (labelled Tar Water!).

A meat bone that is, mostly bone.

He's about to leave when he spies a meat pie.

Pip   Pip, man, ye cannae be takin that!'

But Ah canna leave canibals hungry!

He bolts for the door. Is nearly out and away.

Pip   Bastart! The file!

I'm so sorry, Joe. I'm so sorry kind, loving Joe.

He swipes it and runs like fuck for the churchyard.

Back to the Graveyard

Fog descends, a real pea-souper. Wind howling . . . **Pip** *runs through it terrified. Sprinting with all he has.*

Things suddenly jump at him through the fog as if from nowhere.

Bam! A big rock. Bam! A hedge. Bam! A fuckin goat!

A cow eye balls him. **Pip** *looks ashamed.*

Cow (*or whatever animal you can get hold of!*) Boooooooo (or Baaah! etc).

Pip Honestly mate, it's no fir me, it's no fir me, Ah swear.

Cow Save it for the judge, ya wee fanny!

As the cow disappeared out of sight, back to her foggy dimension, **Pip** *turns back around to get up a head of steam in the right direction.*

Pip Fuck up. Leave me alone. You're no even real!

But before he can focus on anything, without warning . . . BAM!

Crazed Man The fuck are you?!

Pip The fuck are *YOU?*

(*To audience.*) But no sooner have these words shat forth from my mouth than I know. I know it's him. The other guy. The liver eating guy. The monster.

Fuck.

Pip *freezes stiff. Turns to look – the man has gone.*

Pip *is as relieved as he is surprised. He doesn't hang around and scurries off too.*

As he runs, the mist is starting to clear and he can see his original monster.

Pip *approaches him slowly.*

Convict YOU! You came!

Pip   Yeah . . . of course I did.

Convict   Right. Good good good good. You brought whittles, right?

Pip   Ah think . . . Ah think so, sir.

Convict   Whit?! Well, either you huv or ye huvnae!

Pip   Ah huv! Ah huv.

. . . Ah think / It's food right, whittles *is* food, yeah?

Convict   yes it's / acht. Just bloody show me.

Grabs it. Breathes it in more like a dog than a man.

He tears at the food and bites the stone bottle as he drinks.

Pip   Woah woah woah!

Convict   Am I a horse? Then don't you fuckin 'woah' me!

Pip   Sorry, Ah don't mean tae be . . . hingy . . . It's jist . . . that's all there is

and . . . what about the other guy . . .?

Convict   What other guy? The fuck you talking about?

Pip   The guy that wants to eat my heart and /

Convict   / Oh. Aye, that guy . . . eh . . . don't worry you can relax he's gone, aye, he's long gone.

Pip   But I just saw him.

Convict *stops cold, bolts to life, grabbing* **Pip** *by the front of his shirt, looking all around like a startled owl.*

Convict   You what? When? Where?!

Pip   Like literally just a minute ago. He was right over . . . well . . . Ah can't tell exactly 'cause eh the fog but it was literally a minute afore Ah saw you.

Convict   Shit! Fuck. Shit!

Pip Why are you . . . you seem scared . . . is he . . . Please promise me he won't eat me. Please! I did everything you asked. I brought it all. I stole for you even though I'm gonna go to the hulks for it and I'm gonna go to hell and I did it for you and you promised.

Convict I promise he won't eat you.

Dead man can't eat anyone.

Pip You're going to . . . kill him?

Convict No. No. No no no . . . (*Considers it.*) No . . . I'll get him caught. And *they'll* kill him. Death by hangin'. That's what he'll get. That's what he deserves. Justice.

OK, you get away. Run now and don't turn back.

Pip Thank you. Thankyouthankyouthankyouthankyou!

Pip *turns to run.*

Convict Wait!!!

Pip *turns back round, certain he'll now meet his doom.*

Pip Aw naw, please don't kill me.

Convict What? No! The file. You ain't gee'd me the file!

Pip Oh. Oh yes, right, sorry, sorry sir.

Convict Stop bloody saying sorry and give me the bloody file!

Pip Alright, yes, sorry, here you go.

Convict Right. Now you can fuck off. Go!

He starts filing at his leg, this sound can be heard as **Pip** *runs all the way home.*

Pip (*to audience*) On the way back there's no cow's judging me, no goats givin me snippy looks.

And best of all, there's no police at the door to cart me off to the hulks. There's nothing. Just the most ordinary, remarkably calm scene.

Mrs Joe *bursts in to rob the place of its serenity.*

Mrs Joe   Come here, ya wee shite!

She whacks him repeatedly with tickler.

Pip (*to audience*)   Well, remarkably calm for us, anyway!

Mrs Joe   Where in the name of your mother and father's joint grave have you been?!

Pip   I was eh . . . down at the square hearing the carollers singing.

Mrs Joe   I'll sing you a carol, ya little shit.

Pip   Aw, that would be . . . genuinely lovely.

Mrs Joe *whacks him!*

Mrs Joe   Away and boil yer heed, ya cheeky shite.

Now, go and get dressed, we've got guests coming!

Pip   And merry Christmas to you too!

Mrs Joe   You whit?!

She chases him off.

Christmas Dinner

To the sounds of Christmas music, **Mrs Hubble** *and* **Uncle Pumblechook** *take their places and a table laden with food and drink arrives in front of them.* **Joe** *and* **Pip** *haven't changed but put on paper hats.*

Pumblechook   This. Is. Divine, Mrs Joe!

DEEEEEvine!

I tell you.

I tell you now.

I do say.

I do. I say.

I so say.

I say so.

If I have ever had a better pickled leg of pork in my life then I must have sustained a greater kick to the head from that Clydesdale than the doctors first suspected because I can remember no pickled leg of pork, no not one, that surpasses the excellency, the exquisitness, the exceedingly extraordinary exceptionalism of this pickled leg of pork that I have am currently contentedly consuming.

Mrs Joe   Oh, Uncle Pumplechook, stop.

Pumblechook   No

Mrs Joe   Stooop

Pumblechook   I will not

Mrs Joe   You muuuust

Pumblechook   I won't

Pip (*under breath*)   Aye, but you maybe just could though, eh?

Mrs Joe   Well you're too kind. You're too kind.

Pumblechook   Not at all. Not a bit.

Not one teeny tiny bit am I being too anything.

And it's the least, the very very very least I can do to convey my gratitude. My great, grovelling, grandiloquent gratitude for this most unsurpassively unctuous indulgence. Mrs Hubble, will not you support my praise.

Mrs Hubble   Aye. It's unctuous.

This delights **Mrs Joe** *very much despite being comically underwhelming.*

Pumblechook   And Mrs Hubble, would not you agree at this fantastic feast is a sensorial delight for the soul?

Mrs Hubble   I believe it's what the folks on the footballl terraces might call

An absolute belter

A wee stoater

A right wee beltin stoater eh a beezer.

Pumblechook   Well, there you go.

Mrs Hubble (*an aside to no one really as she looks around the table*)   Any more sherry?

Mrs Joe   Really, your gratitude is appreciated.

Pumblechook   Well, you have to ask yourself who wouldn't appreciate such delights? And then . . . you look at him. This . . . boy.

Does he even realise what an honour it is to be granted the right to merely observe this level of highly intelligent reperté and banter from some of the most highly established high heedjuns of high society?

Mrs Hubble   I don't think so.

Pumblechook   Indeed. Look at his face. Pale and glum. It conveys nothing of gratitude. It conveys nothing but . . . well, Mrs Hubble, how would you describe it?

Mrs Hubble   I believe it's what the folk at the alehouses and fighting holes would call . . . glakit.

Maybe . . . gormless?

Dippy? Bird brained? Hawfitted.

Not to mention dunderheaded.

Pumblechook   Yes. Yes, yes, yes. A witless, dunderheaded, slow and imbecilic, bird brained, hawfitted, dopey moron.

Mrs Hubble   Look, let's not be beating around the bush any longer.

We're being too kind.

This woman has done her best.

But let's face facts and call it as it is.

He is what the finest doctors would call.

Well . . . just a . . . stupid lookin bastart.

Pumblechook   At the end of the day, there is a level, with people.

Isn't there?

A maximum level which people can reach in life.

And for him, well, his level is . . . very low.

He's more like a . . . like . . . like a dog . . . with hands.

Now that's unfortunate.

And in spite of all of this you do too much for him /

Does he appreciate it?

I think not.

Mrs Hubble   Ingrate.

Joe   Now, Uncle Pumblechook, I must say, I think you're wrong.

Pumblechook   Oh, do you now?

Joe   Yes I do.

Pumblechook   Oh, please elaborate.

Joe   Oh, sorry, I don't think I could elaborate,

I'm a blacksmith, remember, not a magician.

Pumblechook   Oh, sorry how silly of me to forget.

Well then, perhaps instead of elaborating, why don't you expand on your thinking about how I'm wrong?

That should be fun.

Joe   Well, ye see, you're saying Pip aint grateful, but I thinks he is.

I've heard him say he's grateful.

He's full of grate, aint you, Pip?

Pumblechook   Is that so? Well well well, I stand corrected, Joe.

Joe   That's alright, Uncle, you weren't to know.

Good old **Joe***, he doesn't see when people are pulling station over him or trying to embarrass him.*

Pumblechook   Tell me, Joe, how is the blacksmith trade these days?

If you ever have any money to spare and would like to know which stocks and bonds to invest in just ask and I'll be happy to advise.

Joe   Oh, I don't bother with all that, Uncle. Seems to me that you need to be very smart, a bit reckless and rather greedy to get ahead in all that. We have a roof over our heads, some coal for the fire and the occasional nice thing like a trip to the fare or. Or

Pip   . . . Or the occasional superb dinner of a leg of pickled pork and greens, a pair of stuffed and roasted fowls not to mention pies and puddin's and the like for guests who claim to have a firm grasp on what it is to be grateful and yet are here they are proving the very opposite to be true.

Pumblechook   Erm. I . . . Eh . . .

Joe   Aye, that, Pip. And I'm sure they are, grateful, like. As grateful as me that I can provide it for them.

Mrs Joe   You two be nice to Uncle Pumblechook! Or I'll . . .

She realises she is in company and gathers herself.

. . . would anybody like a drink?

Joe   Oh I should say that would be very nice indeed.

Mrs Joe   Not you! Ya hollerin' walloper. Them.

Pip (*to audience*)   Here, see if they wurny here, she'd eh smacked him for that. I don't exactly know what that says but I think it's worth pointin' it out.

Mrs Joe *gets the jug from the shelf – the jug that* **Pip** *had diluted earlier.*

She fills the glass for each of the guests. None for **Joe**.

Mrs Joe   Enjoy. Right, Ah'll away and get the pie.

She heads off stage.

Pumblechook   A pie?! How delicious! How delicious indeed!

Let's drink to that wummin's good health.

He takes a drink. His reaction is preposterous to begin with and escalates from there. He spits the drink out. He is dramatically choking.

Tongue out, eyes bulging, he rolls around the floor. He is gasping.

On his feet now, which seem to be on fire. Is he trying to shake a hamster out of his trouser leg? He bounds around the room, holding his throat and bounds out the door. Everyone is stunned. While this is going on, **Pip** *speaks to us:*

Pip (*to audience*)   OK. So now I've killed him *and* she's going to discover a missing pie. I am, as they say, fucked.

The door goes. **Pip**, *in a panic, gets up to open in.*

(*To audience.*) Right, plan is – let him back in so he can squeeze out his last breath on the floor.

And while everyone's makin a fuss over him I'll leg it.

And by the time she's remembered the pie's missin'.

I'll already be hawfway tae Auchentoshan.

But it's no Pumblechook. It's

Sgt McLunstry   Sgt McLunstry!

Look sharp. Come with me.

Pip   Alright, fair cop.

He raises his hands is if for cuffing.

Pip (*to audience*)   Ah'd run but a cannae. There must be fifty to a hundred soldiers out there, and if the budget were permittin' Ah'd show you. But Ah can't. So, as it is, you'll just have to trust me.

Mrs Hubble   What's going on? There must be fifty to a hundred soldiers out there.

Pip (*to audience*)   Told you!

Sgt McLunstry   I am here on behalf of the king.

Joe   The king?!

Sgt McLunstry   Yes. Short fellow, wears a crown? I am here because /

Pip   OK OK I'm sorry it was /

No one has noticed **Pip**.

Sgt McLunstry   / the king needs a job doing. I need a blacksmith.

Joe   Oh yeah.

Pip   Oh . . . yeah?

Sgt McLunstry   There's been an incident. We need these shackles fixed.

Joe   Sure thing. For the king, my goodness!

Should be able to get them sorted for you first thing in the morning.

Sgt McLunstry   It's for the king.

Joe   I know, what an honour! I assure you, it'll go to the top of my list.

Sgt McLunstry   Not the morning, not as soon as, not at the top of your list.

It's now. Otherwise it's treason.

Joe   OK, how about you give us . . . seven minutes?

Sgt McLunstry   That's more like it.

Joe *leaves.*

Sgt McLunstry   He's not been drinking has he?

Mrs Hubble   No, unfortunately it all got drunk by one of the other guests.

Sent him a bit doolally and he ran out, you might have seen him?

Sgt McLunstry   Ah yes. Handsome chap (*It's the same actor, you see.*)

Mrs Hubble   Is it convicts, Sergeant?

Sgt McLunstry   Aye. Two. You aint seem them 'ave ye?

Pip   NO!

They all look at **Pip**.

Mrs Joe *comes running in.*

Mrs Joe   Somebody will hang for this!

Officer. Officer! Come quick. Some bastart's nicked ma pie!

Sgt McLunstry   You what . . . sorry?

Pip   Aw what? Oh no. Ah. Aw oh no. Terrible. What a . . . grrr.

Mrs Joe   What are you going to do about it, Officer?!

Sgt McLunstry   Well, Madam the thing is /

Joe *returns.*

Joe   Here you go, Constable. Good as new. Better even.

Sgt McLunstry   Madam, I'm sorry but I must go and attend to this business.

But I give you my word, I will solve this!

Thank you, sir.

To the Marshes!!!

Voices off stage – To the Marshes!!!

Joe   Awe here, can me and the lad go with them?

Pip   Eh, Ah'm no wantin' anywhere near that bin fire!

Mrs Hubble   Ach go on.

Seein a couple eh wronguns gettin malckied' might be good fur ye.

Might make ye less . . . whatever *this* is.

Mrs Joe   Fine. Go if you want! But see if he comes back killed to bits, or with his head blown to pieces by a musket, dinnae be lookin tae me to put him back thegither again!

The Search

Back to the foggy marshes.

As the search takes place, **Pip** *hugs in close to* **Joe**.

Pip   Joe, do you think we should forgive bad people for the things they do?

Joe   Ah Pip, I don't think there's such a thing as 'bad people'.

Just people that's done the wrong thing.

Pip   Joe, would you forgive me if I ever did the wrong thing?

Joe   Ah Pip, just you focus on doing the right thing and you'll be OK.

Pip   . . . OK.

Omnes   *A WHISTLE. Shouting. Many more whistles.*

Sgt McLunstry   CONVICTS AHOY!!! MOVE IN! SURRENDER YOU TWO.

Joe   It's happening, Pip!

Pip   Hide, Joe! They might run this way and . . . knock us over.

Joe   No chance of that. Look, they're not running at all.

They're just beating the Christ out of each other.

We see a shadow fight of two men fighting – puppetry backlit possibly . . .

Sgt McLunstry   Right. Break it up. NOW!

Convict   Ah caught him. You saw, didn't you? Ah caught him and Ah kept him here.

Young Cannibal   Did he fuck, he tried tae kill me.

Convict   Tried tae kill him my arse. If Ah wanted him dead he'd be dead. And Ah could eh been gone. Could eh been long gone. But Ah stayed tae catch him. That makes me a hero.

Sgt McLunstry   That makes ye fuckin' stupit!

Cuff 'em, boys!

Pip   Pleasedon'tseemepleasedon'tseemepleasedon'tseeme pleasedon'tseeme.

Fuck!

Convict (*seeing* **Pip**)   Aw here, Ah need tae tell you something else.

Pip   Aw fuuuuuck.

Convict   While Ah was out Ah took some food frae the blacksmith's down the way.

Some bread, a bit eh booze and a pie.

Pip   You fuckin. You what?

Sgt McLunstry (*to* **Joe**)   There you go. You tell your wife, I'm a man of my word.

I keep my promises. Another case solved by Sgt McLunstry!

Convict (*to* **Joe**)   So you're the blacksmith then?

Joe   Aye.

Convict   Well, Ah'm sorry to you then, for eatin' yer pie.

Joe   Ach yer alright, man. Dinnae worry about it. Look, Ah don't know what ye've done to get ye in this trouble but we wouldn'y want tae see ye goin' starving cause eh it, would we, Pip?

Pip   Erm . . . eh. Eh, no. No, we wouldny, Joe. Not at all.

Good old Joe.

Convict   Oh, and eh. I took this too.

Hands him the file.

Joe   Well, cheers for returning it. Good man.

Sgt McLunstry   Take him away.

Visual moment – eyes meet then **Convict** *is slowly taken away, military sounds and orders? . . .*

Omnes   To the hulks!

Pip   And then he

just

floats

away.

Brief musical interlude and visual moment of time passing.

Time To Get a Job

Pip (*to audience*)   And slowly over the next few years I think of him less and less.

I mean he's always there!

Convict   Boo! Ya fuckin . . .

Pip   Up there. But somehow I push on. So let's erm . . . let's push on.

Right so I'm twelve now, right and Ah might no look it, but I am becoming. A. Man.

That's right. Because. I. Am. Gettin'. A. Job.

Pip   Mrs Joe. Mrs Joe, Ah've been thinkin' about what you said about me needing to get a job and Ah'm thinkin maybe Ah'll be a vet! Or . . . a doctor! Or an inventor. That invents . . . inventions!

Mrs Joe   I'll invent you ya . . .

Ah didn'y raise you by hand so you could have . . . dreams!

Plus. There's no need for them

Because I . . . though I don't know why Ah bother,

I'm honestly too good for you . . .

Ah've already found you a job.

Pip   Wow!

Mrs Joe   Multiple jobs, actually.

Pip   Double wow! Thank you! That's

Joe (*trying feebly to lower his expectations*)   Pip, man, Ah wouldny /

Mrs Joe   You'll go to Mrs Mckecknies and pick the stones out her garden.

Joe   / get yer hopes up?

Pip   Eh? Is that? Is that . . . a . . . a job?

Mrs Joe   It is for you!

Then you'll go and stand in Mr Ha'pennies' field while he looks for his scarecrow.

Pip   Could Ah no just help him find the scarecrow?

Mrs Joe   Well then *who* (*Whack!*) would *scare* (*Whack!*) the *crows*?!

(*Whack whack whack.*)

Pip   Sorry!

Mrs   Right. And when that's done /

Pip   / Bloody hell!

Mrs Joe   You'll to go to the Mrs McLachlin's.

All the waens have stood in dog shit.

Pip   But I /

Mrs Joe   / Take a good stick! And while you're pokin' and pickin' at all the grooves you can maybe have a good think about how lucky you are.

Joe   Well, listen . . . if it's disciple-ing and responsimahingwy he's needin'.

Then . . . Ah could do with a hand in the forge and he could learn the trade.

Pip   Oh my . . . Mrs Joe! Mrs Joe, please! Please! That would be so . . . (*Squeals.*)

Mrs Joe   Do you not think it's bad enough I married a blacksmith?

Let alone raising another by hand!

What would folk say?!

Pip   What would they say about you raisin' a jobby scrapin' scarecrow?

Joe   Go on, it would be good for us both. Please?

Mrs Joe   No. These jobs pay.

Joe   Ah well Pip, at least you'll have a few bob.

Pip   Oh my. So I will!

I'm gonna get . . . . . . (*Scans mind for all possibilities.*) SWEETS!!!

Mrs Joe   I'll sweets ye! It'll go in *there*! (*Big jar on mantle.*)

And you can start workin back the debt of being raised by hand!

Pip   How many jobbies is that?!

(*She whacks him repeatedly.*)

Joe   OK, OK, how about when he's finished all those important jobs, he can help me in his spare time?

Mrs Joe   OK, fine, but only when everything else is done.

And if he's quiet about it!

(*Whack!*)

Pip   OW!

Mrs Joe   I said quiet!

(*Whack!*)

Pip *does an excited silent scream!*

Mrs Joe *heads off.*

Joe   We're gonna have so much fun, Pip. My . . .
apprentice!

*To the rhythm of blacksmithing music . . . shovel, shovel . . . bang,
bang . . . hiss, hiss!! . . . A daft fun '***Pip** *learning to be* **Joe***'s
Apprentice mentorship' montage.*

We see a cycle of the following, all just a couple of seconds each:

*It's clear that as well as learning, they are larking on the job and
having a great time.* **Joe***'s making fireballs and making sparks fly
for* **Pip***'s amusement. But it shows time passing and* **Pip** *learning.
Growing. Flourishing.*

Him sweeping and helping **Joe** *carry things. Him standing in a
field. Arms out. Him picking at a shoe, rushing back to help* **Joe***,*
Mrs Joe *chasing him with tickler,* **Joe** *demonstrating a skill,* **Mrs
Joe** *slapping down a dull-looking piece of bread and* **Joe** *sneaking a
thirteen candle on to it. Will repeat until the 'cake' says he is fifteen.*

Joe   OK Pip, you're fifteen now and it's time for you to
make something.

Pip   Aw wow!

Joe   And it might no seem that big a thing.

But it's probably the most important thing I'll ever teach
you.

You might go on to make intricate jewellery or mighty
weapons (though please don't).

But I'm gonna show you how to make something even
better.

Pip   Magic wand? Skeleton key to the jail?

Joe   I'm gonna show you how to make a . . . nail.

Pip   Oh.

Joe   It's not pretty, it's not glamorous,

but it's something people will always need.

So if you can make a nail, you'll always be OK.

So when times are quiet,

If I'm in between jobs.

Or I just need a moment to myself,

I come out here and I pound one out.

Pip   Joe, I don't think . . . ach, nothing.

Joe   I like the process.

Gives me control.

Stops me worrying about the future. Helps me focus on the here and now.

Which is all there really is, really.

Remember that, Pip:

you're here now.

And that's all that really matters.

A beat. He starts. He is fast. Matter of fact. Mechanical.

OK. Now. While it's hot you want to form the tip

Then move fast and light up the sides to even it out

Hitting it a bit harder now as it cools

Place it in the nail header

A couple of taps and then . . .

WHACK it like all fuck.

He does this. It's quite something.

Equal measure extreme power and routine.

Brute force without emotion.

Pip *certainly takes notice.*

Joe   Right, your turn.

Pip   What? I. Eh . . .

Joe *slips in to routine; hot metal out the fire.*

Places it on the anvil.

Grips **Pip**'s *hand round the hammer.*

and hammers with him. Again it is at pace.

Pip *has to get on board.*

He does. He tries his best.

Joe   It's OK. Shake hands with it.

Good grip.

Right, good tip, Pip.

OK. Good, good, right we'll pop it in there.

Now whack it.

He tries.

Come on, Pip, really give it welly.

You've got strength in there.

Don't fear it.

Look, most scenarios in life require a bit more thought and consideration.

But this?

No. Not this. Ain't nothing else for it but sheer, brute strength.

Go on. Go On Pip. GO ON. YES!!!

Good! Good. Let it all go.

Breathe.

It's done.

You're here. That's all that matters.

Pip (*to audience*)   See right here in this wee moment, I'm happy.

I am, I think about tellin' Joe right there and then, about the convict business. 'Cause I know he'll forgive me. I think.

Convict   Aye but . . . what if he dusnae? OR what if he *forgives* ye, but he maybe loses just a wee bit eh trust in ye? Just enough tae change things so that he stops lookin at you like *that*.

Pip   Fuck, that disnae bear thinking about.

So I leave it. And then Joe turns to me and says

Joe   It's awrite this, aint it?

Pip (*to audience*)   Which for aw the fancy language in the world, and Ah should know cause Ah've heard and used a lot in, especially in later years, there was never a more honest, complex and yet brilliantly simple statement than Joe saying that.

'Cause while he's sayin:

Joe   It's awrite this, aint it?

Pip (*to audience*)   What he's really saying is . . .

Joe   This is contentment, Pip.

Right here, right now.

Sure, there may be a world out there full of thrills and rushes,

and you can spend the rest of your days and money chasing after them.

But there's no need.

'Cause see deep down?

All you'll ever be chasing is this wee bit here.

That moment where it's all, awrite.

Pip (*to audience*)   but of course he doesn't say any of that. He just says

Joe   It's awrite this, aint it?

Pip (*to audience*)   and he is right. So Ah say

Pip   Aye Joe, it is alright. It really is.

(*To audience.*) Ah could eh stayed in that moment for / ever

Mrs Joe   / Where the bloody hell is that boy?!

She grabs him and drags him across the stage by the ear.

To in front of **Pumblechook**.

Mrs Joe   Eejits, the pair of you. There's work to be done.

I didn't raise you by hand so you could lay around like a simpleton.

Pip   Well, we were actually just /

Mrs Joe   / Don't talk back to me in front of Uncle Pumblechook!

(*Whack. Whack. Whack.*)

You see how he talks to me?!

Pumblechook   Vulgar.

Pip   Vulgar?

I was trying to describe a nice moment.

Pumblechook   Talking back is vulgar in any form! A verifiably vulgar and vile vocation.

Now straighten up and listen to your sister when she talks to you.

Mrs Joe   Thank you. Now, shut up and listen up, your Uncle Pumblechook, he has something to tell you.

Pumblechook   Not that you deserve it but I have news of an opportunity that has come your way.

Mrs Joe   You'd better be bloody grateful to your uncle!

Pumblechook   Indeed he should. Though, knowing him, I suspect he shan't.

Mrs Joe   Oh, he shan, he shan be. He bloody better be.

You hear me, you'll be grateful. Won't you, Pip?

Pip   Well, what's the opportunity?

Mrs Joe   Neveryoubloodywellmindwhattheopportunityis justyoubebloodygrateful!

It's a lot more than you bloody deserve.

AND, I'd imagine, *ever* so slightly more prosperous than being a part time scarecrow and a bloody blacksmith.

Pip   But I like being a /

Mrs Joe   / Shut up and listen.

Pip   I'm sorry.

(*Whack.*)

Mrs Joe   Stop (*Whack.*) apolo (*Whack.*) gising!

Pip   Sorry!

Mrs Joe   Shut. (*Whack.*) Up. (*Whack.*) And. (*Whack.*) Listen. (*Whack.*)

Pumblechook   Pip, due to my considerable contacts and connections in just about every field imaginable from bovine to equine matters.

Pip   So . . . animals then?

Pumblechook   I am occasionally privy to certain opportunities.

And, because of the respect I hold for your sister, I have found an opportunity for you.

Have you heard of Miss Havisham?

Pip *is clueless.*

Pumblechook   Well, you ought to have heard of her.

She's quite the respected lady of means.

Joe   Miss Havisham up town?

Pumblechook   Do you know of a Miss Havisham downtown?

Joe   Eh . . .

Pumblechook   She's looking for a young boy to go play at her house.

Pip   That sounds well suspect.

Pumblechook   And thanks to your sister's connections /

Pip   / You mean, you

Pumblechook   you have now been called for to fill the position

Pip   Me?! What the . . . when would I fit it in? I'm . . . I'm happy here.

Pumblechook   What right have you to speak of happiness, boy?

Mrs Joe   Happy?!

You wouldn'y know happy if it battered you with the back eh a spoon!

Pip   I don't want to go.

Pumblechook   Well I am very disappointed. Very disappointed indeed.

Perhaps I should offer this to Mrs Mawhinney's boy,

The one with the bad leg.

He's a very grateful lad.

Very grateful for all he has.

Which, I must say, is not a lot.

He puts you to shame, Pip.

To shame!

Mrs Joe   Would you please excuse us, Uncle Pumblechook?

They move about a foot to the side.

YOU WILL GO TO THAT WOMAN'S HOUSE

AND YOU WILL PLAY.

Pip   But I'm scared. It sounds scary.

Mrs Joe   I DON'T CARE IF IT'S FULL OF SNAKES AND GHOSTS. YOU'RE GOING!

DO YOU UNDERSTAND?!

(*Whack. Whack. Whack. Whack. Whack.*)

Pip   Why would I want to play with an old woman?

Mrs Joe   Because she is insanely rich and wants you to. OK?!

Joe   I'm not sure he wants to /

Mrs Joe   / Enough from you. I don't care what he wants.

This boy's fortune could be made with Miss Havisham.

He's going!

Now come here and get ready!

Pip   What, now?!

Mrs Joe   Naw, Ah thought Ah'd send you out to milk Mrs McGilvery's cow before sending you on this opportunity of a bloody lifetime.

Yes now, ya doss prick!

Vigorous washing music . . . She grabs him like an an eagle pouncing on a lamb and the follows a hilarious and ridiculous scene plays out where **Pip** *is rag-dolled by his sister through wooden bowls and sinks and water pumps to get him clean. He is scrubbed and polished and soaped and towelled and thumped and harrowed and rasped like he was being dragged through the cogs of a machine built for cleaning a car rather than a boy. But somehow it more or less works and he is stood at the end of it all spick and span and pressed and cleaned and in a suit too small and too stiff that he can't really move in.*

Pumblechook   Now THAT'S more *like it*.

Mrs Joe   Well, hopefully she'll recognise the effort.

Right. Be gone!

Pumblechook   Now!

Pip   Eh . . . bye Joe

Joe   Bye, Pip old boy and god bless!

A New Beginning?

They travel to Satis House in awkward silence.

Pip   So . . . I . . .

Pumblechook   Nope . . .

Pip   But I . . .

Pumblechook   Nuh uh . . .

Pip   It's just that I

Pumblechook   Seven times five!

Pip   Sorry, what do you /

Pumblechook   / Seven. Times. Five.

They return to silence until . . . they arrive.

Pumblechook   Pip. This . . . is Satis House!

Pip   This is a . . . house?

Fuck me, it's huge!

Ye could fit our wee hoose in between the gate and the front door.

In fact, Ah reckon could fit every single building Ah've ever been in in ma life – ma house, the church, that wee school, the wee shop, that barn that got set on fire, somehow, all eh them, inside just the hallway eh this place. Unbelievable.

(*To audience.*) And I tell you it really fills out round the side there, goes on for ages.

Pumblechook *takes a look at his watch and looks pompously proud of himself.*

Pumblechook   Punctual as ever.

Pip, it is of the utmost importance that you gain the attribute of being a punctual person. Tell me, what time were we due to arrive?

Pip   Eh . . . quarter past eleven?

Pumblechook   And what time is it now?

He shows **Pip** *his pocket watch.*

Pip (*tries really hard*)   Eh . . . let me see, so . . . you take the big hand and you . . . and the wee hand is . . . but we don't need that one . . . and it's morning . . . so you . . . minus the . . . and then we . . .

Quarter . . . ah, sixteen past eleven.

Pumblechook   Bloody hell . . . that was you, with your . . . just ring the bloody bell.

They arrive at upstage entrance into interior of house.

Estella   What's the name?

Pip *is dumbstruck.*

Pumblechook   Name's Pumblechook.

Estella   You were due at quarter past?

Pumblechook   Yes, that was . . . we were actually . . . sorry.
It won't happen again.

This is Pip!

Estella   Is it?

Pip   It is! Eh. I am!

Fuck!

Estella   Come in then, Pip.

Pumblechook *goes to follow them but* **Estella** *turns and eyes him
which is enough to stop him in his tracks, suddenly fearful of being
put in his place*

Estella   Oh, were you hoping to see Miss Havisham too?

Pumblechook   Erm . . . well . . . eh, if Miss Havisham would
like to see me.

Estella   Ah, but you see she doesn't.

Pumblechook   Ah, right, erm (*Cough.*) very well. That's

eh . . .

Pip (*to audience*)   That's an absolute. Belter!

Pumblechook *leaves.*

Pip   Sorry, erm . . . he's not . . . I'm not with . . . sorry, erm
. . . I'm Pip.

Estella   Yes, I know that.

Pip   Aye. Eh. Sorry. Ah meant to ask you what your name is.

Estella   OK, then why don't you?

Pip   Eh. I don't know.

Estella   OK. Well are you going to ask it now?

Pip   Eh . . . yes!

Estella   OK . . .

Pip   Oh. Yeah. Aye . . . sorry, eh . . . what's your name?

Estella   I'm not telling you.

Pip (*to audience*)   Oh for f (*Trying not to swear.*)

They wind up a stair or head down a big hall or through a big double door or some other way to show that they have entered the faded grandeur of **Miss Havisham**'s *massive house.*

Pip *feels really out of place . . .*

Bust Head   You don't belong here.

Moose Head   Look at the state eh you!

Bust Head   And you'll never belong here

Portrait   Another wee fud come to play!

Pip (*to the objects*)   Oh fuck up!

Estella   Pardon me?

Everything snaps back to place. Normal. Reality.

Pip   Eh, nothing. Sorry.

They pass a portrait of **Estella**.

Pip   Ah ha! Your name's Estella.

Estella   How'd you know that?

Pip   Read it.

Estella   You can read?

Pip   Aye, look, it's here, under your drawing.

Estella   That . . . is a portrait.

Pip   Aye, but somebody's drawn it though, right?

And this word Satis I keep seeing.

What does that mean?

Estella   Enough

Pip   Sorry, I just thought I'd ask /

Estella   / No, boy, it's Latin for enough, it's the name of the house.

Pip   Should've called it . . . more than enough, eh?

Estella   Really?

Pip   Well it's huge.

Estella   Maybe to a common boy it is.

Pip   Well I just think that, as a name /

Estella   / Enough

Pip   I know I know, you told me that, I just /

Estella   / no, that's enough now.

Bust Head   Ha ha, ye wee fanny!

He notices a clock.

Pip   I think all your clocks might have stopped . . .

Estella   Stand up straight you're about to meet Miss Havisham. Do you understand what an honour that is, especially for a . . . common boy like you?

Estella *moves toward* **Miss Havisham**'s *stairs.*

Pip   Oh, eh . . . after you?

Estella   Ye shitin' yerself?

Pip   Ye what? No. I was just. What? No, I just mean. After you.

Estella   Oh, I'm not joining you.

Pip   Oh. Right. OK.

Estella   Unless you would . . . would you like me to join you?

Pip   Well . . . I guess . . . yeah, that would be . . . yeah. Sure, that would be great.

I mean, if you want to.

Estella   Ah but you see I don't.

She strides off, head held high.

Pip   That place, I'll never forget the first time I /

Miss Havisham (*from top of spiral staircase*)   Who is it?

Pip   / Jesus! Eh. Sorry. It's eh . . . Pip . . . Ma'am.

Miss Havisham   Pip? What Pip? Tell me of a Pip.

Pip   Eh . . . from the Gargary's Forge. You sent for me to play.

At least I think it was you. You are eh . . . Miss Havisham, yeah?

Miss Havisham *makes her descent down the stairs from her chair aloft.*

Miss Havisham   Enough, Pip. Come closer, I want a better look at you.

Look at me . . .

What's wrong? You look scared.

You're not scared of a little old lady, are you?

Pip   No. I'm not . . . oh god . . . scared.

No. I'm just. Nothing.

Hi.

Nice to meet you.

Miss Havisham   Come closer, Pip.

He edges ever so slightly closer.

Come on, Pip . . . Closer than that.

Right. Close. Up.

He's right up beside her now.

That's better. Hello, Pip.

Now. Tell me . . . You scared now?

Pip   . . . No.

Miss Havisham   Good. Good good good.

As she talks, her candle catches a cobweb which catches light and burns bright like a fireball before fading. This makes them both jump. But it seems like it was possibly thrilling to **Miss Havisham**.

Miss Havisham   Oh my! Nearly went up in flames there!

Couldn't have that.

That would be a disaster.

Wouldn't it?

Wouldn't it?

Pip   Yes!

Miss Havisham   Yes. Now. Tell me this.

What . . . is this?

She points to the left of her chest.

Pip   It's, erm, it's your heart, Ma'am.

Miss Havisham   But do you notice anything particular about *this* heart?

Pip   Well, I can't really tell from / here

Miss Havisham   / BROKEN!!!

IT IS BROKEN! CAN'T YOU SEE???!!!

This hangs in the air.

Pip (*tentatively and sincerely*)   I'm sorry to hear that, Ma'am.

Is there a way to fix it?

This causes her to laugh.

A little at first, but it builds and builds into a wild and and outrageous cackle. Hard to tell if she is forcing it or gripped by a genuine dark pleasure, but it is certainly uncomfortable.

At it's peak she drops it all in an instant. And . . .

Miss Havisham   No.

Distract me.

Go on . . .

Pip   Eh . . . how do I / ?

Miss Havisham   / Pip. Sometimes I get sick fancies.

Sick little fancies indeed.

And right now I have a sick little fancy that I would like to see some play.

So . . .

Play.

Pip   Eh . . .

Miss Havisham   PLAY!

Pip   OK. Sorry. Erm . . .

Pip *is clearly thinking with his body.*

The panic, uncertainty and indecision is rife in him.

Miss Havisham   Play! Play! Play!

Pip   Eh . . . Sorry, I, erm . . . Do you want a thumb war?

Miss Havisham   A thumb what?!

Pip   . . . War . . .?

Miss Havisham   No.

Pip   Rock, paper, scissors?

. . . Slappy?

Miss Havisham   What are these things you are saying, boy?

Pip   Oh. Slappy? It's a game.

It's quite fun. I play it with Joe.

You both put your hands out like your praying and you each take turns to try and slap the other person's / hand before they pull

Miss Havisham   Pip! I am an old woman.

Who has not seen the sun since before you were born.

And for entertainment, you suggest . . .

Slapping my feeble bones.

It is not just I, then, who has the sick fancies.

Pip   No. It's eh . . . fun.

Miss Havisham   If that's fun, I pray to Zeus I never see your idea of anger!

Have I brought the wrong boy here?

Pip   No. I don't know. Mibbe.

I'm sorry, it's just, this is all new and unsettling

and Ah feel a bit nervous and . . . sad

Miss Havisham   New and unsettling for him

old and familiar for me

he is nervous. I have nothing to fear.

But sad. Yes sad. He and I both.

Yet he does not play.

Pip   Yeah, I know but . . . there's no toys.

Miss Havisham   Then get Estella!

Pip   Estella? The girl that brought me here?

But I don't know where she is.

Miss Havisham   Then you need to call for her.

He goes to the door and calls.

Increasingly louder and more desperate each time.

Pip   Estella.

Esteeeellla.

ESTEEEEELLLAA!

Estella *breezes in with a look of disdain.*

Estella   Yes?

Pip   Eh. You've to play with me.

Estella   Oh, have I?

Pip   Eh, I think so, aye. She sai / eh. Miss Havisham said so.

Miss Havisham   / Estella, I would like to see you play cards with this boy?

Estella   With this common, dirty, labourer boy?

Pip   Oh aye, none taken.

Miss Havisham *leans in close to* **Estella**, *shows her a jewel*

Miss Havisham   This will be yours if you break his heart for me.

Pip   Sorry, what was that?

Estella   You mind your tongue.

And mind your ears.

We will play cards. That's if you know any card games.

Pip   I do, aye. I know three.

Estella   Wow! Three? My goodness! I'm impressed!

Well . . .

Pip   OK. Let's see . . . well, there's Beggar My Neighbour?

Estella   How uncivilised. What are the other two?

Pip   Well, there's erm . . .well, there's Twisted Nipple and, eh, Bash the Bishop.

Estella   OK. So I guess we're playing Beggar My Neighbour then.

Miss Havisham   Beggar him, Estella.

Beggar him!

They set up for a game of cards.

Miss Havisham *sings a wee song to herself.*

Miss Havisham   There will be play, there will be play

My oh my, there will be play.

Pip   You know the rules, yeah?

Estella   Yes, I think I'll manage.

Pip   Right, OK, it's just you said it was a common game and therefore it sort of implied that it was beneath you, and so I wasn't sure you'd have much of a chance to play.

Estella   Well, I *know* that the quickest way to kill a man

is to get a knife behind the wind pipe

and to pull forward through the jugular.

I don't have to have done it very often to know that. Do I?

Pip   Eh . . . no.

You can go first.

They start, she is very quickly trouncing him.

Miss Havisham *is raising different numbers of fingers to tell* **Estella** *what cards* **Pip** *has without him knowing.*

Pip   Bloody hell. Oh, hold on, ah ha!

A jack. Look. At last!

Estella   A jack? Jack is the name of a boy.

These are knaves! Ha ha ha.

But judging by your hands, I don't suppose you'd know that.

Pip   What's wrong with my hands.

Estella   Not as much as your feet.

Or should I say 'hooves'?

Pip   I don't have hooves.

Miss Havisham   Pip, come here, closer. Tell me, what do you think of her?

Pip   I'd rather not.

Miss Havisham   Pip, she says so much of you and you say nothing of her?

Pip   I'd really rather not.

Miss Havisham   Oh, Pip, dear, I must know, just a little, teeny tiny whisper in my ear.

Pip   OK. I . . . think she is . . . nice /

Miss Havisham   Oooooooooh.

Pip   / BUT, she's being a little mean and insulting and I don't know why.

Miss Havisham   Maybe she . . . likes you, Pip?

Did you consider that?

Pip   Well, I mean . . . she's . . .

Miss Havisham   'Very pretty'? Yes, Pip?

Pip   Well, aye. But /

Miss Havisham   / Very good, Pip. Back to playing now.

Pip *does nothing.*

Miss Havisham   No? Is there something else?

Pip   Eh, yes, Ma'am.

Miss Havisham   What is it?

Pip   I think I'd like to go home.

Miss Havisham   Go home now? Well. If you go home now, you'll never come back. And if you never come back, you'll never see Estella again.

Estella, you'd like to see Pip again, wouldn't you?

Estella   Well.

Miss Havisham (*shooting her a look*)   Wouldn't you?

Estella   Yes. Very much so.

Miss Havisham   There you go. Your choice, Pip.

Pip   I didn't say I didn't want to see her again.

I would just like to go home.

Miss Havisham   You'll go home when it's time to go home.

You'll finish the game first.

Pip   Yes Ma'am.

Game resumes. It doesn't take long before **Estella** *has won.*

Pip   Beggar me!

Estella *does a wee victory dance* (*over the top victory dance!*) *she shows what looks like joy.*

Miss Havisham *gives her a signal.*

Estella *leans in playfully, pointing to her cheek.*

So he slowly leans in for a kiss.

Just before he anticipates contact

Miss Havisham *gives another signal.*

Estella *pulls away.*

Pip *falls forward and scuds his head off the table.*

Miss Havisham   Much much work to be done here, Pip before you can match Estella.

A long looooooong way to go.

But I see potential in you.

OK, you can go now, boy.

Pip   Ma name's Pip.

Miss Havisham   Very well . . . Pip.

You've done well here, Pip.

We'll see you soon, Pip, won't we, Pip?

Pip *is unsure but then* **Miss Havisham** *encourages* **Estella** *to encourage him.*

Estella   Won't we?

This is enough to bring him on board.

Pip   When?

Miss Havisham   Let . . . me . . . think . . . when?

When, when, when, when, when /

Pip   / Are you . . . are you saying Wednesday?

It's Wednesday today, so maybe / next

Miss Havisham   / Uh. Uh. Uh. Uh!

Dearest Pip.

I know nothing of days

I know nothing of weeks

I know nothing of years

Arrangements will be made

I will be here. Estella will be here.

Now go. Go.

Pip   OK, I'm going!

Pip *is visibly starting to cry.*

Miss Havisham   Estella, take him down.

Estella   Gladly. Come on. Let's go.

Once outside the room:

You know the way from here. Don't you, boy?

Oh but before you go,

I'd like to show you what a real loser looks like.

Theres a mirror just up ahead. Haaaa!

Estella *skips off stage left to do a fast costume change into* **Mrs Joe**.

Pip *almost cries again but just about pull himself together. As he heads down the corridor, he has to pass the mirror.*

Pip *turns away from it, sad, looking at his hands with shame.*

Pip   Stupid. Stupid. Stupid.

You're just, you're just AAAArgh.

Just a RRRRRGGGH.

Stupid, common, filthy, stupid, useless, stupid boy.

His crying and hyperventilating passes and he slumps in the floor.

Pip (*to audience*)   I never wanted to set foot in that house again. And I never wanted to see Estella again.

But I instantly wanted to turn back and be with her again.

This *feeling* I felt . . . I had no name for.

Like . . . *all* the feelings at once. And all of them horrible.

And yet. *yet* . . . I just wanted to look at her and say 'I'm here, you see me, right?

Say something nice about me. Please.'

I wanted her to like me. So much.

Pip Returns Home

Pumblechook *is waiting expectantly.*

Pumblchook   Well, boy.

Tell us. Detail. Did you behave in a manner expected and befitting?

Pip *looks him up and down.*

This beast is no better than him. He takes a deep breath and as calm and controlled as you like he says

Pip   Three times five!

Pip, *with all the power, starts to walk away until* **Mrs Joe** *comes running in.*

Thrashing him around between every question.

Pip *hardly able to muster a response, all the while getting more flustered.*

Mrs Joe   OK, Pip, tell us straight. Did you do well?

Tell me you did well?

You better have done well!

Pumblechook   Your sister, what raised you by hand asked you a question.

Mrs Joe   Oh he'll have fucked it up, the useless bag of shite.

Pip   No, Ah didn't fuck it up, actually! They said I was great, actually!

Said I had load of potential. Actually!

Mrs Joe   Well that's . . . OK tell us more!

Pip   Why don't you ask him what it's like inside Miss Havisham's.

I'm sure he could tell you loads.

Pumblechook   She asked about your day, not for a guided tour!

Pip   But you could tell her what it was like, couldn't you?

Pumblechook   Of course I could!

Pip (*to audience*)   Well, if *he* can lie, so can I!

Pip   OK. Right! So, as we entered

I was treated to steak and chips

from the chef in the main hall

while they sized me up for proper pair of boots for the . . .

Pumblechook *is desperately trying to interject to look like he can corroborate and 'prove' he has been treated to similar experiences.*

Pumblechook   Horse riding.

Pip   Yes. And I was such a natural that they put me on this special horse, it had black and white stripes.

Pumblechook   That'll be the zebra, yes, she had it imported from . . . Spain.

Pip   Zebra! That's right, Pumblechook, you know it.

Pumblechook   Oh yes, Pip, fine beast.

Pip   Fine. But how it kicks.

Pumblechook   Yes.

Pip   And bites.

Pumblechook   Oh how it bites.

Pip   And with such sharp teeth as well.

Pumblechook   So sharp!

Pip   More like dogs' teeth.

And so many dogs there as well.

Great big ones. Doing all sorts.

Back flips.

Riding bikes.

Joe (*arriving*)   They sound amazing.

I hope she treats them well?

Pip (*feeling bad for the first time*)   Don't you worry, Joe.

She treats them very well.

They have their own chef.

Pumblechook   Such a dog lover she is.

Mrs Joe   She sounds lovely.

Pip   Yes. And very wise. And very witty. And very generous.

Mrs Joe   And the place? What was the place like?

Pip   Grand. So grand. Aint it, Pumbly?

Pumblechook   Yeah, very grand indeed.

Pip   And so much gold, eh?

Pumblechook   So much.

Pip   It's gold this, gold that. Gold

Pumblechook   Forks.

Pip   And ch. ch . . . chai . . .

He's playing with him now, the arse.

Pumblechook   Chairs.

Pip   Oh, I was going to say chains on the toilet.

I didn't know about the gold chairs.

Sound really fancy.

Pumblechook   Oh so fancy.

Pip   A bit cold though, maybe.

Pumblechook   Eh . . .

Mrs Joe   What else? What else?

Play? What did you play?

Pip   Well she lets Dunfermline Athletic train on the back court

So I got a runaround with them.

Mrs Joe   Oh, he's to be a sports star.

Joe   Well, he said Dunfermline, but . . . still.

Mrs Joe   Either way there could be a reward here!

Pumblechook   Yes. Property most likely.

Mrs Joe   Or money perhaps or a gold chair we could sell.

Joe   Or maybe even one of these beautiful dogs!

Mrs Joe   If you've nothing sensible to offer then go make a nail!

Joe *starts heading off.*

Pip   I'll come with you, Joe.

Joe *in the forge.*

Joe   Whatever your sister says, Pip, I should very much like to meet these dogs.

Pip   Joe, man, I need to tell you something.

Joe   Is it about the dogs?

Pip   Kind of, yes.

Joe   Oh, fantastic, you can tell me anything about these dogs.

Pip   They're not real, Joe.

Joe   Well, apart from that, I guess.

Pip   Sorry, Joe.

Joe   No great dogs?

No dogs at all?

Not even a single one?

A puppy?

Oh come on, Pip, a puppy?

Pip   No. I'm sorry. I made it all up. All of it.

Joe   You lied, Pip? Why would you . . .

Pip   I don't know, Joe!

It was a horrible day.

And a horrible place.

They were rude to me.

And there was a girl and she was . . .

I was dead nice to her and she called me common.

Joe   We are common.

Pip   I know. I know. But. With them, that felt like a bad thing.

And then I got back here And. Pumblechook's *worse* than them.

And I didn't want him to know I was sad.

So . . .

The **Convict** *enters.*

Joe   So you lied.

It sounds tough, Pip but

If you need to lie in order to be with these . . . uncommon types

Then maybe you're best to just stick with us common types.

Convict   Ach he doesny get it, man. He doesn't understand!

Joe   If you can't get to being uncommon through going straight, you'll never get there going crooked.

Convict   You are crooked!

Joe   So tell no more lies, Pip and you'll live well and die happy.

Pip   You're not . . . angry?

Joe   What? No! My goodness, Pip.

Why would I be angry?

Pip *is genuinely relieved.*

Joe   Speaking truthfully, I'm a little disappointed.

This is deflating though.

But I'm glad you told me.

Pip. I think it's important to own your shit.

It's the stuff of life to make mistakes.

That's no cause for anger.

Come here, Pip.

Joe *opens his arms for a hug.*

Pip *runs at this act of kindness.*

He really, really needed this

Joe   Pip. You might be common in some ways

But you're uncommon in many others

You're uncommonly . . . bright.

Convict   You're uncommonly weak.

You're uncommonly stupid.

Joe   And you may use these things *for* or *against* yourself.

But, Pip, just know this. You *are* enough.

You are enough. You remember that, old friend. OK?

Pip   OK, Joe.

Thank you.

Joe   That's alright, Pip.

Best of friends you and I.

Now off to bed.

Pip's Dream

Pip (*to audience*)   Sleep did come. But when it came it was brutal.

Pip *wrestles around in the sheets.*

Estella *appears.*

Estella   You're dreaming about me, Pip.

Pip   Naw I'm no!

Estella   Yes you aaare.

Pip   I'm not!

Estella   Yes you are, Pip.

Pip what do you want?

Pip   I don't know.

I just want you to be nice to me.

Estella   Pip . . . Have you got. A pinger?!

Pip   NO!

Estella   Yes you haaaave!

Pip   AH HAVE NOT!

Estella   Yes you do.

Pip   I don't! I don't, I don't . . . Ah . . . don't get pingers
yet!

This was the wrong tactic. There's an explosion of laughter.

Estella   Whooooahh haaaaa

*Every available character (especially **Pumblechook**) appears to
laugh at him.*

All   Haaaaaaa

Pip *jumps out of bed.*

Pip   Just shut it the lot of / you.

Estella *hands him a mirror.*

*His reflection appears in the form of another person pretending to be
him.*

Estella   / Aye, that's right, that's you. Loser.

Ya manky, dirty, useless, common nothing of a boy.

Pumblechook   No better than live stock.

Estella   You're right. Look at those hooves he calls feet.

Pumblechook   And that skull. Did he get it from a quarry?

Joe   Don't listen to them, Pip, you're uncommonly bright.

Estella   Don't listen to him. He calls knaves jacks.

Miss Havisham   You've a long way to go, Pip. A looooong way.

Estella   What nice things could I say to you?

Miss Havisham   A long looooong way.

Convict   You just gonna take this, Pip?

What are you going to do about it, eh?

Omnes *laughter.*

All   What you gonna do?!

What you gonna do, eh?

Pip *is awake. All dream stuff gone.*

Pip   I'm gonna fuckin . . . show them!

Laughing crescendo leading to . . . End of Act!

Act Two

Pip's *getting ready and heads to Satis House and appears in front of gauze before the reveal of the banqueting room.*

Pip (*to audience*)   This is it. I'm gonna show them. (*Brushes hair.*) I'm gonna show them what I can be! (*Shines shoes.*) I'm gonna get smart. (*Straightens collar.*) I'm gonna go far in this world. I'm gonna show them all. Gonna /

Estella *joins him in front of gauze.*

Estella   / Could you not have washed?

Pip (*bubble burst!*)   But I . . . I did wash!

Estella   / Hurry up! Well?

Pip   Well, what?

Estella   Do you think I am pretty?

Panic!

Pip   Erm . . . Eh . . . Well . . . Yes.

Estella   Alright, creep. And tell me, am I mean? Am I insulting?

Pip   Eh . . . well, maybe a wee bi . . . no. No, not really

Estella   Not really? OK. OK . . .

Are you just going to go up and tell it all to her instead?

Pip   No! I . . . I . . .

Estella   Oh why don't you cry again . . . pig boy,

Pip   No! You'll never see me cry again!

Estella   I will!

Pip (*to audience*)   She does.

Estella   I told you to hurry up!

Music plays as the room is slowly revealed through gauze and gauze is rolled up . . . the cobwebbed wedding banquet.

Estella   The boy is here, mama –

Estella *runs off leaving* **Pip** *isolated.*

Miss Havisham (*voice from somewhere*)   Is that it? Is that what six days feels like.

Enter and wait for me.

The room is a decaying freeze frame.

A rotting meal is set on a long table and in the middle – a giant cake, crumbling, moulded, rat bitten.

Pip *takes it all in.*

Miss Havisham, *enters quietly behind him, puts her hand on his shoulder.*

Pip *shits himself.*

Miss Havisham   This is where they will lay me to rest

Right here on this table

This is where their eyes will feast on my decaying flesh

She points at the cake.

Miss Havisham   Do you know what that is?

Pip   Mould?

Miss Havisham   Beneath the mould. What does the mould devour?

Pip   I don't have a scooby!

Eh, I couldn't possibly say.

Miss Havisham   It's a cake.

Do you know what kind?

Pip   And old one?

Miss Havisham   It is a wedding cake

MINE!

It was brought to this room many years ago

There were plans for a feast

But it has decayed in here

And I decay in here with it

And when the decay is complete

They shall lay me here in this bridal gown

And the curse upon him will be complete.

(*A change of direction.*)

Pip. What do you dream of?

Pip   A horse.

With knives for hands.

It chases me through a field

And then I fall face up in a pool of jam

He slowly closes in on me

Gets his big horsey face right in mine

And hes just about to slash me to bits with his knife hooves

when I wake up.

Miss Havisham   In life, Pip. What do you dream of . . . in life?

What do you want to be?

Pip   Be? I am. I'm Pip.

Trainee blacksmith.

Miss Havisham   WHAT DO YOU WANT FROM LIFE?!

Pip (*terrified*)   I . . . erm . . . I don't . . . know

Miss Havisham   Do you want . . . love?

Pip   Yeah, sure, of course, that would be nice

That would be really nice

Miss Havisham   Oh yes? And who would you like to love you?

Someone like Estella?

She starts one her little laughs that turns to a big cackle.

Before again stopping abruptly.

Miss Havisham   Walk me.

Pip   What, sorry?

Miss Havisham   Walk me!

They walk around the room in awkward silence.

Well, awkward for **Pip**. **Miss Havisham***'s in her element.*

Finally.

Miss Havisham   Pip, if you're to have love,

You'll need to have ambition.

You'll need to offer them something more than a miserable, turgid, existence.

Pip   Well, I think that if you're nice to people, then /

Miss Havisham   ESTELLA!

She enters.

Estella, come here.

Tell me, what do you want from life?

Estella (*as though she is running lines to please* **Miss Havisham**)

Great things. Many great things

And someone great by my side

Someone who does great things

Holds a great position

And is greatly respected by people

And then I . . . crush / them.

Miss Havisham   / Ah. AH. Ah . . .

Tell me, is a blacksmith great?

Estella   I wouldn't think so.

Miss Havisham   So, you would want better than that then?

Estella   Yes. Better than that.

Miss Havisham   OK, thank you, Estella, you may go.

She leaves.

Miss Havisham   See boy? See.

Pip   And so. How do I be better?

Miss Havisham   Well, that's something we shall have to work on, Pip.

OK?

Pip   OK.

(*To audience.*) And so this is what we did then most days. Walking. And her talking. Telling me I need to improve in just about every aspect of life. Me going home, workin' as hard as I can with Joe, and stayin up reading book after book after book to get as smart as I can. Learning about the world and showing off to her.

Occasionally I'd get to play with Estella, but moments with her were kept to minimum. And even though every time I never got more than a

Estella   Look at the state of you.

Pip (*to audience*)   Or . . .

Estella   I thought you were meant to be . . . 'improving' yourself?!

Pip (*to audience*)   Or a . . .

Estella   How, when you say you work as a blacksmith, do you smell so much like a farm?

Pip (*to audience*)   These wee moments kept me going. From autumn into winter, into spring into summer. Same every day.

Apart from one time when, as I'm leavin', I notice this guy. He's scrawny. Scrawny as fuck like. Looked like he couldn'y lift his own socks to put them on. But he also had that air about him that suggested that no one would ever make him lift his own socks.

Pocket   Want a fight?

Pip (*to* **Pocket**)   Do I want a . . . sorry, did you just . . .

Do I want a fight?

Pocket   Yeah. Do you want a fight?!

Go on. Fight me!

What's wrong, you scared?

You scared of . . . this!

Pip   Scared? Nuh!

Naw man, I just . . . don't think we should /

Pocket   Ha ha. You're shittin' it. You're shittin' it. Ha ha!

Pip   Listen mate, I'm not shittin' it.

(*To audience.*) OK, I'm kind of shitting it. But just like.

(*To him.*) Right, listen up you . . .

Pocket   Go on then, put them up!

Pip   Hawd on, man, I just don't think we / should

Pocket   / Now, come on, you've been given fair warning for a fair fight so you'd better stick em up.

Pip   The fuck is this guy's problem.

Pip, *tentatively puts 'em up. It is laughable. He is as uncertain as* **Pocket** *is comically confident – winding up one way, winding up the other. Stepping back and forth on the ball of his foot. Make no mistake, as ridiculous as it is,* **Pocket** *is not playing the laugh, he is committed, completely unaware of how ridiculous he looks.*

Pocket   Three . . . two . . . one

There is not even a beat to be had between 'one' leaving **Pocket**'s *mouth and* **Pip**'s *fist connecting with his nose, it was instinctive, reflexive, a prize horse out the traps, a sprinter from the blocks and so before* **Pocket** *can even consider is first ridiculous bob or weave, he is a crumpled heap, his nose exploded.*

Pip   Fuck me! You alright?! I didn't mean . . . sorry! . . . Ah just . . . It was . . .

Pocket (*dazed*)   It's eh . . . just . . . ooft . . . just . . . give me a . . . ooooft . . . minute. I . . . . . . A good strike indeed. But I am not ready for this to be (*He climbs slowly to his knees then feet.*) over

Pip   Listen man, you cannae, we cannae /

Pocket   What's wrong? Scared I'll exact my revenge?

Pip   No. I'm just . . . I don't want to / (hurt you)

Pocket   Nonsense. A lucky strike. Now put 'em up!

Pip   Man, this is nuts, we cannae be

Pocket   Three!

Pip   Fuckin hell

Pocket   Two . . . one!

Pocket *manages the tiniest of movements that that could be potentially classified as defensive, before . . .*

Pocket   Ah ha, see you're not so /

. . . BANG, an exact repeat of before. A single smash and he is wiped out. **Pip** *is as bemused as* **Pocket** *is destroyed. He staggers to his feet and away.*

Pip *stares at his hands in a state of shock and horror before running off.*

Estella *has watched the whole thing and is impressed.*

Miss Havisham *has continued to walk round the room as if* **Pip** *is still on her arm.*

Pip (*to audience*)   So, aye, apart from *that* mad moment, it was pretty much just all the same old routine. Until finally . . .

Miss Havisham   Pip. Let's get serious.

What is your plan here?

Pip   OK. Well . . . erm. I

Miss Havisham   Tell me!

Pip   OK. So, I've been working really hard. And studying even harder.

And . . .

I'm going to be the best blacksmith there ever has been

And the smartest!

Miss Havisham   Pip. Being the world's smartest blacksmith

Is like being the worlds cleanest pig . . . (*She gives up.*)

Do you genuinely want this life of nothing with . . . Joe?

Pip   Well, it's honest. And we have a laugh.

And I figure this way I get the best of both worlds

I can be happy *and* be a gentleman.

Miss Havisham   Pip.

Have you *any* idea the sheer gap between even

the *highest* paid blacksmith

and the lowest rung of gentleman

that might be good enough for someone like Estella?

Listen to me now, Pip.

The kind of love you will find

Living the life that you are right now

is the kind if love fit for dogs and pigs.

Sweating and grunting through miserable indifference until you die

If you want love, any kind of real love

If you want anyone to love you

then you had better become something!!!

Pip   I . . . I . . .

Miss Havisham (*cutting him off*)   Bring this Joe to me

Pip   Joe. Here? . . . OK.

Joe Meets Miss Havisham

Joe *looks around incredulous as he walks into the room.*

Joe (*aside to* **Pip**)   Bloody hell, Pip. This's a house if ever I saw one.

You could lose a hippo in this place!

Pip   Nah. You'd hear it. It's really quiet in here.

Joe   Ah, but what if it was sleeping?

Pip   I think they snore quite a lot

Joe   Dead then

Pip   OK.

Joe, come here, can I just /

He takes a moment to try to smarten **Joe** *up.*

A straighten of the bowtie, a levelling of the sleeves.

A dust of the shoulders.

Utterly hopeless.

Pip   Ach that'll do.

C'mon.

They are in the room.

Miss Havisham   You will be Joe then?

Joe   I *am* Joe . . . *now.*

Miss Havisham   And Pip is apprentice to you?

Joe   Yes, Ma'am.

Miss Havisham   And you are happy with this?

Joe   As happy as a pig in sh . . . Shetland.

Best of friends we are, Pip and me.

Miss Havisham   And Pip is happy with this?

Joe   I think so.

Though you'd need to ask him.

Pip, you having a good time?

Pip   I am. Yes. It's just /

Miss Havisham   Just . . .

Pip   Just that . . .

Miss Havisham   Alright, Pip, I'll make it simple.

Do you want to come and live here, learn the ways of the world?

Gain respect of your elders and betters?

Or do you want to go full time with Joe and learn the ways of
. . .

I want to say . . . a lathe?

It's your choice.

Pip   Well, Ma'am I . . .

Miss Havisham   I need clarity here, Pip.

Certainty.

Some things in life will require thoughtful consideration,
debate and discussion.

Not this.

This requires brutal honesty.

Sharp distinction.

Absolute clarity.

Pip   I . . . I . . . It's just . . .

Miss Havisham   / Well that's pretty clear to me.

Pip will end his time here.

And he can commit to being your apprentice.

Here is his money for his time here so far.

It's not his fortune. But it's more than handsome.

I had thought more of Pip.

But he obviously doesn't think enough of himself.

Pip   Sorry, but I would just like to say that I /

Miss Havisham   Say goodbye, Pip. Say goodbye to it all.
Say goodbye to Estella.

Pip   Erm . . . goodbye, Estella. I . . . will I see you again?

Estella   Well, unless you happen to be invited to the Mayor's Annual Gala

Or I happen to be invited to the weasel fighting championships

At the Pig and Whistle then . . . no, I wouldn't have thought so.

Pip   I . . . I . . .

Miss Havisham   / Be gone now.

Pip and **Joe** *leave*

Joe *in delight. He marvels at the money, the house, the whole thing.*

Joe   Astonishing. Astonishing. Astonishing. Astonishing.

Pip. You could do absolutely anything you want with this money!

Busker *is playing a tune . . . walks up to* **Joe** *and* **Pip**.

Busker   Ah'm sorry brothers but there's no a chance you could spare me enough to get a sausage supper and a bottle of ginger.

Joe   You know what my dear fellow man

Pip   Joe . . .

Joe   Ordinarily I might not be able to help out.

But it just so happens that today is a good day.

And therefore a lucky one for you.

Pip   Joe!

Joe   Well, lucky for you as long as Pip here doesn't have any obsessions

Pip   Well, no, it's just /

Joe   Because I hope he remembers that if we help others when the going's good, then the going is better for all and therefore even better for us.

Pip   / Aye, yeah, you're right. Go on.

Joe *gets the money out.*

Busker   Fuck me, that's a tidy sum.

Joe   Indeed. And you're very welcome to your bit and there enough in there for a pickled onion or two as well.

Go strong friend.

The **Busker** *stares at the money this could go either way.*

Pip   Joe ('come on . . .')

The **Busker**, *overwhelmed, has a bit of a cry.*

Busker   My god, you're a good man. A bloody good man.

Joe   So are you man. Go strong. Go strong.

Now back at the house. **Mrs Joe** *and* **Pumblechook** *are there.*

Mrs Joe   Well? How did it . . . Oh . . .

Oh, ye've fucked, haven't ye. Ah just knew ye'd fuck it.

Pip   Well congratulations, you were right. I fucked it. Well done you!

Pumblechook   Well, it can't be helped. As I said, there is a level with everyone

And for some people it is . . . very low.

Pip   Ach . . . rammt, Pumblechook!

Forging Ahead

In the forge.

Joe   Oh never mind them, Pip. Here we are. At last, just you and me.

Full time.

Some laugh we'll have pip. Some laugh.

And there's no time like right now to crack on wi the rest of your life so let's erm . . .

Pip   Forge ahead?

Joe   No, Pip. Come on, the forge is round the side.

You must know that, you've been in there enough to know that.

Pip   No, Joe, I know where the . . . it's 'cause eh the two meanings eh forge. Like where you work but also like . . . pushing ahead. So, eh . . . never mind.

Joe   Two meanings? My god, I never knew.

You could eh been a scholar, eh Pip?

Pip (*this has caught him off guard but he tries to chum along like it hasn't*)   Aye . . . maybe.

Joe   Well, what does all that matter when you're so happy here?

Pip   Aye, what does any of it matter?

Never mind, eh?

Joe   Aye, never mind, Pip!

Let's . . . forge ahead, eh?

Brilliant. What laughs, eh Pip, what laughs.

A wee montage of **Pip** *and* **Joe** *working away in the forge.*

Joe*'s doing his best to have fun and amuse* **Pip**. *But* **Pip** *is just going through the motions in a sad and resigned way. The dialogue is in his head and happens over the action.*

Pip   You ever been ashamed of where you're from?

I hope you haven't.

It's a horrible thing to feel.

It's like being ashamed of yourself or something. I would just look around the place and think about how horrible it would be if someone like Miss Havisham or Estella might see it.

Estella *peers in at the window, she is only in his mind.*

Estella   How do you live like this?!

Pip   It's just . . . what I'm used to I guess.

Estella   Ah . . . Ye shat it. Didn't you?

Pip   Naw! It was /

Estella   / You knew that if you'd taken Miss Havisham's money, you'd only have fucked it because you're just a wee common boy and that's your level.

Pip   Naw! It was . . . Ah stayed for Joe.

If it wasnae for Joe, Ah would totally have /

Estella   / Come on, Pip is it not just easier, as the months turn to years, to blame Joe and this place for holding you back than facing the reality of trying and discovering you're just not good enough?

The montage continues. They work. They rest, the seasons change. He will blow out his sixteenth, seventeenth and eighteenth birthday candles. Blown out with a jaded sigh.

Until.

Joe   Wow Pip! Your eighteenth birthday, I'm so proud of you.

Let's knock off five minutes early to get you a glass of rum.

And, there's a quiz on!

Pip   Yay!

Jaggers Arrives in Town

Bar Staff   Whit ye wantin?

Jaggers   Rough talk? How delicious. I'm wantin' . . . is that how I . . . 'wantin'?

Bar Staff   Aye.

Jaggers   Oh, look at me. Well, I am *wantin'* a young boy.

Bar Staff   No that kind eh place.

Jaggers   No no, god no. A specific young boy. Young man. By the name of Pip.

Bar Staff   And . . .?

Jaggers   Oh, yes, thank you?

Bar Staff   Whit ye wantin'!

Jaggers   Oh yes of course. Sorry. Erm, just something simple.

A . . . New York sour.

Bar Staff   Ale or rum.

Jaggers   Which vintage?

Bar Staff   Last week.

Jaggers   Just a short one with plenty of . . . soda? Tonic? Erm . . . lime? Water.

As it is'll be fine. Thanks.

Bar Staff   You daein eh quiz?

Jaggers   Am I Dana? Quiz?

No. I'm Jaggers. General Gerald 'Geronimo' Jaggers

Associate Law.

Bar Staff   No. Are. You. Doing. The Quiz?

Jaggers   Ooh. As jolly good fun as that would be, I need to stay on business.

Bar Staff   Fine. But there'll be absolutely no talking while I'm asking questions.

Jaggers   Right you are.

Bar Staff   Because we have a rule – Anyone talks during ma questions, we will /

Jaggers   / Give me a right good ribbing?

Bar Staff   No. We'll cut your fucking face off. Specifically Wonky Terry will cut your fuckin face off. You're just lucky that when you cut me off there I was merely making an informative statement and not asking a question, or you'd already be without face.

Jaggers   Noted.

He finds **Joe** *and* **Pip**.

Jaggers   Excuse me. But might one of you go / by

Bar Staff   / OK everybody? Question one.

Jaggers *instantly bites his tongue.*

Bar Staff   What was the name of the biggest cow at the county fair last year?

Jaggers (*waits to make sure he is definitely done talking, proceeds*) Sorry might one of you /

Bar Staff   / Question two! If a train leaves Birmingham station travelling at 37 mph. How many whelks did Small Ron eat at the Whelk Off?

Jaggers   . . . one of you go by /

Bar Staff   / Question three. When worming a sheep. How long must you wait before you feed it starch?

Jaggers (*speaking really quickly*)   might one of you go by the name of Pip!

Joe   Ah that would / be

Bar Staff   Question four. If I went to Mrs Mawhinney's butchers with half a crown and bought three bridies, a sausage roll, two mince rounds and a Paris bun. How much change would I get?

Joe   Sorry friend. Can't speak over the question.

He gets a bit . . . slicey.

And that was a long one. Right, so, Pip? Yes, that would be /

Bar Staff   Question five! How many hands are in a foot?

Joe   Sorry. Didn't see that coming.

So, Pip is

Jaggers   Please man, just /

Bar Staff   / That concludes our first round.

Jaggers   Thank god. So you are Pip? You seem older than I imagined.

But the air round here can . . . age one so.

Joe   No, no, no, this is Pip.

I'm Joe, his master blacksmith.

And I've had it said that I look well on my age.

Pip   Aye, he's 106.

Joe   No no no, he joshes, he only means to josh, not lie.

Hate lying. Just a josh.

We have some laughs, eh Pip?

Pip   Aye.

Joe   So what you wanting Pip for?

Jaggers   It's good you are here actually, I must speak to you as well.

Bar Staff   Round Two!

Jaggers   Bloody hell. Somewhere more private please.

The pub disappears –

Right, Joe, I must ask, would you be happy to release Pip from his apprenticeship if it was for his benefit?

Joe   Well, I wouldn't say I would be happy.

Jaggers   Oh well, that's that. That was quick.

Got to see a delightfully frightful pub out of it though

So not a total waste of time.

Joe   Woah. Sorry, I said I wouldn't be happy because I wouldn't.

But I'd never ever step in the way of what Pip wanted to do

Specially of it was for his benedict

But you'd need to ask him.

Jaggers   Well in that case I sit myself back down and turn my attention on you, Pip.

Pip   Ach what's the point? Ah fucked it wi Miss Havisham so I may as well stay here and rot as apposed to going anywhere else and rottin' away. Nah, Ah had ma chance and Ah stuffed it. Ah'm eighteen noo, ma best years behind me.

Jaggers   Well, actually. It is my duty to inform you that you have great expectations.

Pip   Ye whit?

Jaggers   You have great expectations, Pip.

Pip   Naw. Ah don't!

Jaggers   Someone begs to differ. They have seen to it that you will be given a property. And the life of a gentleman.

Pip (*more to himself than anything*)   My god, I . . . Havisham
. . . she must have . . . and for my eighteenth . . . I . . .

Jaggers   The thing is though, young Pip.

That in order to accept this offer, you will need to leave all of
this.

This town. This job. This life.

This is not an decision you can be expected to make / lightly.

Pip   / I'm in. Right now, I'm in. Hundred per cent. I'm in.

Joe   Leave . . .? What will . . . he do for work?

Jaggers   He'll not need to work.

Joe   He won't need to work?

Pip   I won't need to work?!

Jaggers   You'll be given a salary befitting a young
gentlemen of great expectations.

Joe   If he's not working. How can it be a salary?

How can it be honest?

Jaggers   If you have any objections speak now

Pip   None at all

Jaggers   Good. I should think not. There are some
stipulations

Joe   Always a catch

Jaggers   Firstly, the person from whom I take my
instructions says

you must always bear the name Pip.

Secondly, your benefactor wishes for their identity to remain
totally secret unless they decide to reveal it to you.

Even if you think you know who it is, you must say nothing.

You understand me?

Pip   Yes, apart from. Whatthefuckthisismental?!

Jaggers   A lot to take in, I know, Pip. But your life is to change.

He hands him a bag of money.

Joe   Bloody hell!

Jaggers   Impressed?

Joe   Terrified.

Pip   This will change my life. What could I possibly spend all that money on?

Jaggers   That's merely to buy a new suit.

You'll start receiving your salary when you get to my office in the capital next week.

Good night. And fair thee well, Pip.

He leaves.

Joe   Bloody hell, Pip.

Pip   Joe. Did that just happen?

Did that actually just happen?!

Joe   It certainly did, wee man. I can hardly /

Pip   / Fuckinnnn yaaaaaaassssss

Joe   Exciting times, wee man.

Pip   Can't believe it. But, Joe, hold on? What about you? Come with me?

Joe   Ah don't worry about me. I'll be fine.

Pip *swaps his cash for a sharp suit, talking to us as he dresses.*

Pip (*to audience*)   She knew. She knew that I could do it. Long game man. You've done it. You've done it!

Pip Goes to See Miss Havisham

Miss Havisham   Pip. You look . . . different.

Pip   Miss Havisham . . .

I wanted to let you know that I'm off to the capital tomorrow.

Miss Havisham   You go tomorrow, do you?

Pip   So you *do* know?

Miss Havisham   Let's just say that . . . Jaggers is *my* lawyer too, Pip.

Pip   Well, you should know that I am so so grateful to *whoever* my benefactor is. (*Wink wink.*)

Miss Havisham   Yes, your very rich and generous benefactor who I believe, Pip, wishes not to be named.

Pip   Yes, Ma'am.

And I know you can't . . . hingy . . . say if it was you or not.

But I want to check. To ask. If.

Do you really think I can make something of myself?

Miss Havisham   Oh Pip, I think it would be very safe to say that I think you can make something of yourself.

I tried before to keep you here.

And now . . . now that you are eighteen.

A very *wise* person has given you a second chance.

A very wise person indeed.

You will go very far.

Pip   Thank you, Ma'am.

Miss Havisham   Whatever for, Pip?

Pip   Eh, sorry . . . aye, just. Eh. For, well you brought me here and let me spend some time here.

And now . . . *someone* has given me this opportunity

And I can't help but feel that they are linked.

Miss Havisham   Oh, if only Estella could see you now

What a match you two would make.

Pip   Do you really think so?

Miss Havisham   Do I really think so?

Do light waves bend when travelling from one medium to another?

Does the pull of the moon's gravity hold our planet in place and stabilise our tilt?

Do starch molecules form clumps in a béchamel sauce unless you stir constantly to evenly distribute the heat?

Pip   I . . . think so?

Miss Havisham   Then there you go

Pip   Is she . . . around?

Miss Havisham   No.

She's gone to France. To learn.

I hear that every debonair in Paris is chasing her.

But you work hard, Pip.

You take this chance.

You toughen up that soft heart of yours.

Take my advice and cut off ties with home.

Pip   I don't think I could /

Miss Havisham   You saw what happened before.

They held you back, they'll do it again.

Pip   . . .?

Miss Havisham   You toughen up and you make it in this world and you might. Just. Win. Her. Over.

You never know. She may end up in the capital one day.

Pip   She might?

Miss Havisham   She might.

Pip   Thank you, Miss Havisham.

Miss Havisham   My goodness, whatever for, Pip. (*Wink.*)

Pip   You know.

Miss Havisham   Do I? (*Wink wink.*)

Pip   Yes you do.

Miss Havisham (*she waves her cane playfully like a magic wand*)

Your dreams are coming true.

Pip   Thank you.

Goodbye

Pip (*practicing to himself*)   Joe, it's not easy . . .

Joe, I hope we'll stay close.

Joe, I'd stay for you, I would, but I tried that and it's making me

Oh I don't know, I just wonder what's out there and

Joe tell me if I'm doing the wrong thing

Joe I love you, and /

Joe *enters carrying* **Pip**'s *nightcap and teddy for him.*

Joe   / Well, good night then, Pip, we'll be seeing you in the morning.

And we'll walk you into town

So this aint it. This aint the end here.

It's just . . . just goodnight.

So . . . goodnight, eh Pip.

Pip   Good night, Joe.

They hug and head to their rooms, **Pip** *doubles back, checks the coast is clear, grabs his bag and sneaks out the door. He is gone.*

A silence.

Joe *re-enters talking. Carrying a little present.*

Joe   Oh, and Pip, before I forget, 'cause I'll forget,

I made you a little thing.

In the forge.

It's delicate.

Not fancy.

He starts to look around.

But a bugger to make.

It's what they call a cufflink.

Checks **Pip**'s *door.*

Just something to . . . remember

us . . . (*Dawns on him he is gone.*)

by.

. . . Bye Pip.

Live happy, dear friend.

Pip (*to audience*)   For anyone that needs to hear this: It is absolutely alright to cry. Tears are vital. They're a super power. They tell those around us, especially those we love, that we need help. That we care. That we have feelings way beyond the depth of our words or our actions. Never be ashamed of them. If I'd cried sooner I'd maybe been able to stay and say goodbye. To let Joe know I was as scared and sad as I was excited. But I didn't. I cried the whole walk to the coach. And once I had I felt strong enough for a strong good bye. I wanted to go back but . . . it was done now.

Enter horse, cart and **Driver**.

Pip   Sorry mate. Can we turn back. I forgot something?

Driver   OK.

They turn back.

Pip   Actually, just go on.

Driver   OK.

They turn back again.

Pip   No. I'm sorry. I think I do actually need to go back.

Driver   Whatever you need.

Turns once more.

Pip   Shit, no, actually, I think I should leave it.

Driver   Right, this is a carriage ride. Not the fuckin hokey cokey!

You wantin' me tae take ye home or no?!

Pip   No. Drive on. Sorry.

Driver   It's alright, you sure?

Pip   Yup

They drive in silence for a moment.

Pip   Mate, you ever want something so bad that you can't even stop to think about whether or not it's good for you?

And you think that by doing it you'll be giving up

who you are and what you love and what you know

and even though you know you shouldn't

you still want to more than anything?

Driver   Nope.

Back to driving in silence

The Capital

Pip   Awrite, Mr Jaggers?

Jaggers   Aw. Rite? Am I . . . saying that right? Delicious.

But that will need to go.

It's 'Good day, sir' for you from now on.

Pip   Oh I think that sounds a wee bit stuffy for me.

Jaggers   I wasn't giving you options, Pip.

You're to be a gentleman, there are certain rules.

Some written. Some unwritten.

Some spoken. Some unspoken that you must adhere to.

And one of them is not to greet your betters and elders in a manner befitting to someone who's just stumbled backwards out of a fistfight at a dog track.

Pip   Oh. Right.

Well. OK . . . eh . . . Good day, good fellow.

Jaggers   I am Mr Jaggers, sir.

Pip   Sorry . . . Mr Jaggers . . . Sir

Jaggers   So you should be.

Right, as your guardian, I have arranged for someone to train you in ways of a gentleman.

(He calls, extremely loudly.) MARTHA!!!

Martha (*who, it turns out, is sat very close to* **Jaggers**, *as it looks like she always is. Ears ringing.*)   Yes?

Jaggers   Fetch young Pocket.

Martha   Kelvin!!!

He was also very close. Appears now. Ears ringing.

Pocket   Yes?

Jaggers   Pip. This is young Kelvin Pocket.

You will live with him and he will teach you the ways of a gentleman

Pip   But hold on. You're . . . he's . . .

Jaggers   Kelvin Pocket. Yes.

Pip   No, he . . . I . . . battered him

Jaggers   You . . . sorry, what?

Pocket   My goodness me, so you did

I barely recognised you there old chap

Jaggers   If there has been previous criminality I'd really rather not hear of it

Pip   No, not criminality, it's just

Jaggers   You said, and I believe I'm getting this right, that you 'battered him'

Pip   Aye, but if anything, I'm pretty sure I was the victim

Pocket   It's actually rather straight forward good sir.

I challenged him to a fight.

He obliged.

He, ever so slightly, got the better of me

All good.

Everyone is happy.

Pip   Well, I wasn't. I was horrified by the whole thing.

But, glad to see you're well and there's been no damage.

Jaggers   OK. Pip, here is your first payment.

He drops a bag that is much bigger than what he gave him back at the forge.

Pip   Holy f . . . there's enough there to last a lifetime.

Jaggers   Well, maybe your old lifetime, Pip

But you only have to make that last the month, that's your monthly salary

Pip   A month. What in the name eh high speed horse travel am I to spend that on in a month?

Jaggers   Not my concern.

Pocket   I'll show you.

Jaggers   And then you'll get your birthday bonus.

So, really you should never have any concerns about money again.

Now, I recommend whatever you do you leave a bit back for my services

Should you partake in any nefariousness . . . ness.

Pip   Oh, I'll not do that. I'll put it all to incredible good.

I'll not waste any and make only the very best of this opportunity.

Pocket   Why the fuck would you do that, Pip.

You're a gentleman!

Jaggers and **Pocket** *laugh maniacally.*

Pip *chuckles along, confused.*

Pip and **Pocket** *head outside.*

Pocket   Pip. My old boy.

The Bruiser of the Back Court

The Psycho of Satis House

The Nut Job of the North.

Pip   None of that is really how I / am usually

Pocket   / Don't worry about that.

It's good to see you, my man.

Pip   It's eh. It's, aye, it's good to see you too.

Outside they meet man in street.

Man in Street   Here Guv, I don't suppose you've enough dosh for me to get a cup of splosh and a round of toast have yer?

Pip   Well /

Pocket   / Pip!

Pip   Ordinarily I wouldn't be able to help out

But it just so happens that today is a good day for me

And therefore a lucky one for you

Pocket   Pip. What are you . . . /

Pip   / Pocket, you must remember

if we help others when the going's good,

then the going is better for everyone

and then even better for us.

So, good sir, my lucky day is now your lucky day

And there's a little extra for a bit of /

Pocket *grabs* **Pip***'s outreaching hand to block the exchange.*

Pocket   Uh . . . there certainly is not and there shall be no such thing.

Shoo. Shoo now from my friend and leave him alone.

Go. Shoo. Go now!

Man in Street (*leaving, shamed, crestfallen*)   I'm sorry. Sorry sir. Sorry. I just. sorry

Pip   Mate, so am I . . .

Pocket   OK, Pip. We are going to have to toughen you up.

Pip   I battered you.

Pocket   Be that as it may, you still have a soft character

You can't just give a handout to every leech going

Pip   Leech? I think that's . . .

Pocket   Well, he did absolutely nothing to earn the money in your pocket.

Pip   Neither did I!

Pocket   Pip. It's *yours*.

Pip   Right. Good.

Well, there you go.

And I wanted to give some of it to him.

Pocket   Of course. Of course. And that's admirable.

It really is.

I want to help too. Believe me.

We all do.

Honestly.

But really. How does it help?

You help him now and what?

He gets a bed, a meal for the night?

Pip Yeah. Maybe. Hopefully.

Pocket But then what?

This man, if left with hunger and drive could have become the next leader of the free world.

Now? Now he looks for you again tomorrow?

And the next day? And the next . . .?

And then he tells his friends.

And he tells his and it never stops.

Until they've bled you dry.

You can't help them anymore.

They've forgotten how to fend for themselves.

And now they're all dead.

Oh, it might feel good to help but I've just saved you.

From giving him, and all his friends, a death sentence.

Pip Well, I've never thought of it like that before.

Pocket It's alright old chap. You've a lot to learn.

Much work to be done.

Let's go for lunch while I bring you up to speed.

Pip Erm.

Pocket Let us go to Harrods.

You must try the gold encrusted pear.

You've simply never had pear

until it's been encrusted in gold.

Pip I've never had a pear.

Pocket My goodness. Well, just wait till you try the tiger meat!

They do the most incredible cut of tiger meat

stuffed with panda heart

Much, much work to be done, Pip

A long, loooong way to go

We'll soon get you sorted.

Pip's New Property

During following chat, workmen are delivering chair, rug, bottles of champagne etc and **Pip** *absentmindedly signing for them.*

Pocket Right, Pip. You're looking well and you're well fed, but we've a long way to go if we're to get you ready for the Mayor's Gala

Pip Did you say Mayor's Gala?

Pocket I did /

Pip Bloody hell! Right. Teach me everything you know.

Pocket Do you know it?

Pip Yes. And . . . there might actually be . . . a . . . girl I like there.

Pocket Pip. There will be *lots* of girls you'll like there!

Pip No no! It's er . . . just the one.

Pocket OK . . . suit yourself!

Right. First of all, we'll need to fix how you sound. Now, there's really only two options with a Scottish accent down here. And that is go hard or go soft.

If you go hard, you need to push out all your vowels, like you're shouting, but close your throat a bit to bring the volume down.

People *will* understand you but you do run the risk of sounding a little crazed.

So if you take this approach, be sure to be extra chummy with people or they might feel a little threatened by you.

Pip   Halloa. Ma Name's Piiip!

Pocket   OK. A . . . *bit* threatening.

Pip   Hallo. Ma Name's Pip.

Pocket   Niiice. It has an edge but it's workable. Like a chummy janitor or a wild trader.

Right, now, alternatively. If you soften, which I, for the record, do recommend, you need to work the mouth more. Right? Let the vowels lilt over the mouth, which will force you to speak a little slower than before.

Pip   HellooOo Maoy Nayme Iis Piip.

Pocket   Good. Just the right amount of boring.

That will help people take you more seriously.

In fact, they might not even really notice you're Scottish at all!

Pocket, *proud of a job done, leaves.*

Pip *turns to us and speaks in his 'proper voice'.*

Pip (*to audience*)   So, yes, for a while, I spoke like this,

He returns his voice back to normal.

it's not something I'm particularly proud of or keen to dwell on but there you go.

And see when my real voice *would* slip out and I'd get a pure slagging . . . Did I stick up for myself? Did I point out how cruel and alienating it was? Did I batter them? No. I'd laugh and join in so it was over quicker and we could . . . feel like friends.

He looks around his new place.

Ten years! Ten . . . *years* I spent in this place! Oh, a lot
happened. I learned to talk, to dance, to dine, and converse.
I learned to look the part, how to look at art and keep a
portfolio. I learned how to eat. And drink. A lot. I learned to
spend . . . with abandon!

I learned to be . . . 'something'!

It's all a bit of a blur.

Joe would come! Of course Joe would come. Well, more so in
the early days . . .

And I *would* be delighted.

But it would just end up going like

Pip   Joe! Have a drink!

(*To audience.*) And he'd say

Joe   I'd better not

Pip (*to audience*)   And I'd say

Pip   Take some money!

(*To audience.*) And he'd say

Joe   I'd rather not

Pip (*to audience*)   And I'd say

Pip   Go on!

(*To audience.*) And he'd say

Joe   If it's all the same to master Pip, I'd rather not,

Pip (*to audience*)   And I know it probably wasn't but I let
myself feel like it was loaded

And even though I knew he probably didn't, I let myself
believe he resented me

And that made me resent him.

And that made me say things like

Pip   Joe, I wish you would spend the money I sent you on a proper suit then we could go out

Pip (*to audience*)   and he'd look a bit hurt and say

Joe   Well, I'm not very comfortable dressing as something I'm not.

Pip   But Joe, you look like . . . a scarecrow.

Joe   There aint much so wrong with scarecrows, Pip.

Pip   Oh aye, very good, you saying that I'm being something I'm not? Because, actually, I am actually something. Oh Joe, just get over my success would you? Stop trying to hold me back and let me help you.

(*To audience.*) And so there's no surprise really that he's back less and less. but . . .

. . . oh aye and there was the Mayor's Annual Gala. Where I would get to see . . . Estella (*She appears.*) and every year I would try and win her over.

The ball comes to life in full swing.

Pip *works up to making his approach.*

Pip   Estella It is *I* !

Estella   Sorry . . . Who?

Pip   Well, seeing as I never saw you at the Pig and Whistle for the weasel fighting I figured I would have to come and meet you here.

Estella   Pip?! My god. It's nice to see you!

Why are you . . . talking like that?

Pip   Because I am now a gentleman of great means and that means that we can now be together!

Estella   Eh . . . sorry, I . . . that's a bit . . . well. I . . . live in France.

Pip   Oh

(*To audience.*) Which, by the next year, became

Pip   Estella, it is my pleasure to see you again.

Estella   Er . . . nice to see you too, Pip. Sorry I just need to
. . .

Pip (*to audience*)   Which became

Estella   I'm sorry, Pip. It was nice to see you but . . . But I
think . . . I'd better go.

Pip (*to audience*)   And so on and so on over the years while
she was being chased by bastards like Bentley Drummel.

The Gala slows down.

Yeah, they all became a bit of a blur too to be honest. But I
remember the last one.

Yeah, I remember the last one.

I'd have been . . . fuckin' hell. Twenty-eight!

Joe visited earlier in the day.

And it's been so long.

And it's so good to see him. But so hard to say that.

And so I say:

Pip   Joe! Come on in and have a drink!

(*To audience.*) And he says

Joe   Pip, I'd rather not.

Pip (*to audience*)   And I say

Pip   Oh, Joe, if you won't come in and take a drink, why
are you even here?!

(*To audience.*) And he says

Joe   Because I thought you'd like to know that your sister
has parted this world.

Pip (*to audience*)   And *I* said . . .

Pip   Oh come on now, Joe. If there was ever anything to drink to, it is that!

Ach bollocks . . . I'm all out of champagne!

But don't worry. It's the Gala's tonight!

We'll get you done up and we can go out and celebrate!

Oh come, Joe . . . cheer up. She's deed!

She'll be happy . . . At last!

(*To audience.*) And he says

Joe   Pip. There will always be a place for you at home.

But I think it's best I stop coming here.

Pip (*to audience*)   And I say

Pip   Fine. I agree.

He watches **Joe** *slump off.*

Pip (*to audience*)   But I don't.

Pip *drinks and staggers back into the Gala scene, which comes back to life.*

Pip   Estella. You're amazing. And Ah hink Ah'm awrite.

So . . . when we gonna, ye know . . . get married?

Estella   Is this a a proposal?

Pip   No . . . unless . . . is that . . . do you . . .

You're no gonna marry that bastart Bentley Drummell?

Estella   Pip, go drink some water.

Pip   Oh, Estella, are we gonna keep going on like this?

Estella   Like what?

Pip   Oh come on, you know what I mean.

Estella   Do I?

Pip   You know I love you. And that I've loved you since I first saw you.

Since we played and you were so . . . we're meant to be.

Estella   Says who?!

Pip   I don't know . . . fate?

Miss Havisham? She wants us to be together.

Estella   Pip. We only met because Miss Havisham brought you to the house so I could torture you.

Pip   To play.

Estella   Pip. Do you think you were the only one? There were hundreds. I hated it!

But I hated you the most. Because you made me feel sad. At least the others had the self respect to walk away. But you were just so desperate for something, anything, that you just kept coming back. You were a nice lad, with a good heart, but the things she made me say to you, that I agreed to say to you. I hated it. I hated myself for doing it. I prayed you wouldn't come back. In the end I had to beg her to let you go.

Pip   Naw. Naw, she wanted me to do well. And maybe . . . maybe that's why she gave me all this money, because she feels bad and /

Estella   Pip, if she has given you money, which I severely doubt, it's not because she feels bad. She never feels bad. I should know.

Pip   Naw. It's . . .

Estella   Pip, do yourself a favour and let go of that place and all that happened there.

I know I'd like to.

Pip   Well, it . . . doesn't matter how we met. You said I was a good lad. We can still /

Estella   Pip, do you think this is love?

You act like we're destined to be together

But it's been years now

And in all that time you haven't asked a single question

What I like? What my dreams are?

You don't know if you like me.

Pip, mostly you just stare at me.

Do you know how many people I have to put up with staring at me?

He's doing it.

He's doing it.

So's he. And him. And him. (*Lots of faces popping up around stage! And she can point to men in audience as well.*)

You've just done it the longest.

It doesn't make you anything special

Or make us any more destined to be together.

Pip (*staggering off mumbling*)   You're wrong. You're wrong. I became something.

Estella   Bye, Pip . . .

Ball ends sadly – dark music . . . . scene change to **Pip***'s flat.*

Pip Gets a Visitor

Pip *arriving home it's very dark.*

Pip   I am Pip! I'm Miss Havisham's prodigy.

She believes in meeee. I'll fucking show you alllll!

A thud a rattle in the dark.

Hello? Hello? Pocket? Is that you?

Is it Bently Drummell?

You don't scare me, ye bastart.

You ask Pocket, he'll tell ye. I'll box your ears / off

A noise. Definitely from within.

Pip *is scared now.*

OK. Whoever it is, just show yourself.

If it's money you're after, don't hold your breath

(*Tries on a rougher voice for size.*)

Right, listen up, ya . . . bastard, ye,

I will / not

/ *A figure emerges in the shadows.*

Pip *runs for the door.*

The figure blocks it off.

Pip   Heeelp

Magwitch   It's alright, it's alright.

Pip   I beg to differ.

Magwitch   Pip!

Pip   How do you know my / name?

Magwitch   / Pip, it's me – Abel Magwitch!

Pip   Who? What?

Oh god. Oh good god. The convict! No. I'm sorry. I'm sorry.
No!

Please! Please don't eat me!!

Magwitch   Eat you? What the . . . what? I'm no gonna . . .

Why in the christ would I eat you?

Pip.

It's me!

I'm so proud.

Look at you.

Pip   What are you talking about?

Magwitch   Pip. I gave you all this.

Pip   What? No. What are you . . . All you gave me was a deep rooted psychological trauma and the practice of internalising all my pain and anxiety that started with the belief that helping you has booked me a place in hell when I die so I'd better not speak of a word of it to anyone else lest I spend what life I do have before I go to hell in prison.

Magwitch   Christ Pip, that's a lot.

Pip   Yeah. It is!

It is.

Magwitch   Well, Pip, you ain't going to hell.

Pip   Says you.

Magwitch   Pip, you helped a soul in need

That's what gets you sent upstairs

Not down.

Pip   But I stole and I lied.

Magwitch   Why?

Pip   Because you asked me to

Magwitch   Exactly.

I was desperate and I made you desperate.

I'm sorry, Pip.

But know this. I've spent every single day trying to repay you.

Every penny I have made is yours.

And, by fuck, I have made a lot of them.

For Pip, you so deserve it.

Pip   Rest assured I don't need your money, sir.

I have my own money.

Magwitch   Yes, Pip. I've been sending you it for years now.

Pip. I'm your secret benefactor.

Pip   My god, is this stolen money?

Am I living off stolen money?

Magwitch   NO!

It's all honest money

Hard earned.

Pip   Then why are you hiding?

Magwitch   Because I'm not meant to be here.

I was sent to Australia

For previous crimes.

It's death for coming back.

But I had to. I had to come back.

To see you. To see that it has done you well.

That I've done this well.

That I've repaid you.

Pip   You promise me it's you that's given me my money.

Magwitch   I promise.

Pip   Prove it.

Magwitch   I send all I earn to Jaggers and he sees it goes to you.

Pip   My god.

Magwitch   Will you help me?

Pip   If you can stay here till I get back?

Magwitch   Oh man. I aint goin *anywhere!*

Oh, one thing . . . you got wittles?

Pip   . . . There are provisions in the larder.

Magwitch   Ever the kind soul, Pip.

Pip   And if my roommate Pocket comes back

Just tell him you're an old family friend

And for god's sake don't say you'll eat him

I need to go and speak to someone

Taxi!!!

Pip *goes running on the spot – everything swirling around him.*

He bursts in to **Miss Havisham**'s *room.*

Pip   You!

Miss Havisham   And what wind, may I ask, dear boy, has blown you here?

Pip   Don't dear boy me anything.

Miss Havisham   Ooh. He's learned to be feisty on his journeys

I like it!

Pip   Yeah, I've learned a lot. Actually

Miss Havisham   Excellent. How about a little quiz ?

Pip   How about, I just tell you what I've learned, OK?

I've learned the identity of my secret patron.

Miss Havisham   How exciting.

Pip Is it, aye?

'Cause I bet you'd love to know

'Cause it's not you.

But you see, Ah thought it was you.

Miss Havisham That's interesting.

Pip It is, is it?

Miss Havisham Why ever would you think it was me?

Pip Well, ye see, because I think you led me to believe it was you.

Miss Havisham Yes.

Pip Why would you do that?

Miss Havisham Why would I not?

For fun. For play.

I told you when you first came here I wanted to play with you.

Pip Well that's . . . you're . . . not very . . . nice

Miss Havisham Nice? Nice?! Who in god's green earth am I to be nice to you?!

And who in the suffering bowels of hell do you think you are to deserve it?

Nice. Nice?! Nice.

Pip And Estella? When you said you believed that I would become desirable to her. Did you at least mean that?

Miss Havisham Games. Pip.

Games, games, games.

Come on, Pip, seriously?

Oh, Pip. Oh, Pip. You wouldn't really have thought . . .

Oh, Pip.

A classic maniacal laugh builds.

Look at her.

She's . . .

No.

She's to marry Bently Drummell.

Pip (*to himself*)   That bastart?

Miss Havisham   A genuine gentleman.

Pip (*he gathers himself*)   I have wasted enough of my time here.

Miss Havisham   No, Pip. *I* have wasted enough your time.

I have wasted a lot of your time.

A lot of your life.

You and all the others. But you the most.

And I have thoroughly enjoyed it.

Pip *doesn't dignify this with a response.*

He stands strong. Turns to leave.

Oh Pip, don't leave.

I'll miss you

I'll miss our games.

It'll be hell without you, Pip?

Oh, do you want me to be in hell, Pip?

Oh, Pip. What do you want me to do?

Say sorry?

Oh, I'm sorry, Pip.

Do you want me to prove it?

Do you want me to beg?

Do you want me to set myself on fire?

Do you?

She lights a corner of her dress.

Oh, look how it starts. Oh. Ooh.

The fire grows around her.

Oh, Pip. Look how sorry I am.

Look how sorry I am, Pip.

Pip.

She's dropped the sarcasm. Is increasingly panicked.

Piiip.

Pip. I'm sorry. I'm sorry, Pip. Piiip!

Pip. I'm going to hell.

Pip, I don't want to go to hell. I'm sorry!

I'm sorry!!!

Pip *runs back in.*

Tackles her, dousing the flames but alas, it's too late. Something from the wedding feast smashes down . . . for a brief second it appears as if the whole theatre is in flames!

Pip   Taxi!!!

Everything swirls back in reverse to London flat.

Pip Helps Magwitch

Pip (*to audience*)   So, I head back to my flat where, for the second time and with as many nerves but a lighter conscience and more conviction, I try to help Magwitch get away.

But instantly I'm met with Pocket.

Pocket   Pip. I fear we may be in danger.

Pip   You're not, it's fine. He's a friend.

Pocket   He threatened to eat me!

Pip   He . . . what? Magwitch. I told you not to /

Magwitch   / I'm sorry, I'm sorry but it's just . . . really effective.

I'm sorry. I'm sorry. I'm not going to eat you.

Pocket   Pip. Come here.

(*In hushed private tones.*) Did you say 'Magwitch'?

Pip   Yes. Why?

Pocket   His name's all over the town.

My god. He's a wanted man, Pip. He's to hang.

And you'll hang for helping him.

Pip   Well, I'm going to help him.

Pocket   People are looking for him.

There's a heavy reward.

You'd be better doing the right thing.

Pip   Helping him is the right thing.

Pocket   It pays less.

Pip   It often does.

Look, you don't have to help me

but if you can get me a boat,

I'd be extremely grateful

And I'll keep your name out of it.

Pocket   OK, I can get you a boat, but that is it.

I'll play no further part in helping you.

Or him.

*Scene change – dramatic tone . . . stage fills with fog and smoke –
sound of the sea, and sea gulls . . .*

The Great Escape

In complete darkness.

Pip (*to audience*)   It's cold and it's quiet on the harbour. It
had seemed the smart thing to do to steal out at first light
but as soon as we're there I wish it had been busier, to help
us blend in . . .

Pip   Quick – climb in this boat.

Magwitch   We stick out like a burst dick.

Pip   Be that as it may, let's get going.

Magwitch   Pip. I don't like the look of this other boat.

Pip   It's fine, we're just nervous, just keep rowing.

Magwitch   We'd better, Pip, 'cause I'm afraid that, if I don't
make it, there isn't enough to keep you in this life.

Pip   That's OK. I'm not helping you to keep me in this life.

I'm helping you so that you can get the rest of your life.

And when you get there, I want you to enjoy it.

You've sent me enough. And I've . . . wasted it.

This is me saying thank you to you.

Don't you send me any more money.

Or I'll not do you any more bloody favours.

Alright?

You get back home. And you retire.

OK?

Magwitch   OK, Pip. Good lad.

Pip   Good.

You do the things you've always wanted to but never had the chance.

Magwitch   Right you are, Pip. I shall try and find my daughter.

Pip   You have a daughter?

Magwitch   I do, Pip, somewhere. Had her taken off me when she were a babe.

Broke my heart.

Maybe I should finally face that.

Her name was . . . (*Sudden sound of police whistles, dogs barking etc.*)

FUCKING HELL THE ROZZERS!

Pocket (*on dock side*)   There they are officer.

The convict and my friend he's taken hostage.

Pip   Bastart

Magwitch   It's OK, Pip. It's OK.

Pip   What are you doing Pocket?!

Pocket   I wanted the reward, Pip.

Pip   But you don't need the money.

Pocket   I know, Pip. But I like money. And now I have more of it.

Magwitch   It's OK, Pip, if you go with them now they'll not punish you for helping me. I've got it from here.

Pip (*to audience*)   And he dives in

Pip   You'll never get anywhere, you'd not even get back to the dock

(*To audience.*) And I dive in after him.

Magwitch Goodbye

Magwitch *is coughing and wheezing and wet, manacled again and held by an officer.*

Magwitch   Well, Pip, the bad news is I've to spend the rest of my life in prison.

The good news is they say I've to hang on Monday.

Pip   I'm sorry, sir.

I really tried to help.

Magwitch   I know, Pip.

I know, but I'd not say that too loud near him, what with you an accomplice and all that. I'm sorry, Pip.

Pip   It's alright. I did what I did. And I would do it again.

Magwitch   I tried to give you it all, Pip, I did. I tried to give you what you deserved.

Pip   It's fine. I appreciate it, I do. I know you had good intentions

But it's not what I need.

Magwitch   Oh, I'm sorry, Pip. What should I have done?

Pip   I don't know, could you not just have told me that I was good?

And then told me again and again until I believed it?

Magwitch   You are good, Pip.

Pip   I don't know.

I think maybe I was.

But . . . I don't feel it now.

Magwitch   You've got time, Pip.

You're here, and that's what matters.

Alright?

Pip   Alright.

Magwitch *is led away by the officer . . . sad moment.*

Officer   And we'll be speaking to you soon.

Last Trip to Jaggers

Jaggers   Pip. Your payment isn't till tomorrow?

And from what I understand their won't be much more coming.

Pip   I know. That's OK.

How many payments are still due to come my way?

Jaggers   Let me see . . . Seven.

Pip   OK. That's enough for seven lifetimes.

Jaggers   Well, you're old /

Pip   / Yes. My old life. Yes yes.

But that's . . . OK. First, I'd like you to /

Jaggers   / I'd advise you've wait until you've covered your bail, Pip.

Smuggling a death row convict?

You're probably looking six years.

That won't be cheap!

But with my *connections* I think you'd have enough.

Pip   Thank you. But no.

I did what I did. I'll own my shit.

OK. So, first, when my payment comes tomorrow, I'd like you to arrange a proper burial for Abel Magwitch. And if there isn't one at her grave already, a head stone for my sister that reads . . . 'Worked too hard, died too young'.

OK, next.

Tell me. What is the nearest property for sale to Mr Pumblechook's?

Jaggers   Well, as it happens, the house directly opposite is available.

Pip   OK. And how many lifetimes would that cost?

Jaggers   Two – I have the keys to it as it happens!

Pip   And do you have a reliable map to get there from here?

Jaggers   Indeed.

Pip   OK. I'll take it!

Jaggers *hands him a key and a map.*

Pip   Thank you.

And the rest I'd like you to put in trust to Mr Magwitch's daughter

Minus your fee and a fee for someone who can track her down.

Jaggers   As you wish, sir.

Pip   Please, call me Pip.

He heads outside. The **Man** *who wanted a saveloy supper earlier is there.*

Pip   Excuse me, mate.

I want to give you something.

Firstly an apology.

But I know that's not enough. So I want you to have this.

He hands him the key and map.

Man in Street   What? Man. You can't . . .well, luv a duck!

Pip   No questions, no catch, it's yours.

I only have one stipulation.

Man in Street   Sure Guv, anything.

Pip   You make lots of noise. All day, all night.

Get a cockerel. Get an elephant if you can.

Just . . . enjoy it.

The **Man**, *overwhelmed has a bit of a cry.*

Man in Street   My god, you're a good man. A bloody good man.

Joe   So are you, man. Go strong. Go strong.

Pip *heads off.*

He sees the officer from earlier.

Pip *calmly raises his wrists and willingly goes with the officer.*

Six Years Later

Pip, *free from prison and not sure exactly where to go finds himself back at the burnt-out Satis House looking around.*

Estella   Pip? . . .

Pip   My god, Estella, I didn't think / I would . . .

Estella   / I thought you were . . .?

Pip   Got out after five years.

'Good behaviour.'

Estella (*with genuine warmth*)   Well, that's . . . something.

Pip   Aye. Gave me time to think.

Helped me clear my head.

Estella   What are you doing back here?

Pip   I don't know, I was just . . . wandering

And I thought . . . maybe I'd /

Estella   / Check and see if she was still dead?

Pip   Ha! I don't know. Something like that, maybe.

How are you? What are you doing here?

Estella   Living. Trying to. This is mine now.

Pip   And.

Estella   Bentley?

Oh, you were right.

He's a bastard.

Pip   I'm sorry, that's grim.

But I wasn't right.

I didn't know he was a bastard

any more than you

He could have been the nicest man in the world

and I'd have still said that.

I'd have said that about anyone

'cause he wasn't me

and . . . aye. Well, I'm . . . sorry to hear that. I am

And I'm sorry for everything before.

Estella   Thats erm . . . thanks.

And erm. I'm sorry for what I said that night.

Pip   Oh god no.

No, no, no.

I absolutely needed to hear that.

Thank you.

It was good of you.

You deserve to be happy.

Estella   So do you, Pip.

Do you know that?

Pip   I think so.

They look at each other.

Pip   But not . . .

Estella   Together? . . . No

Pip   No. That would be . . .

Estella   A bad idea.

Pip   A very bad idea, aye.

Estella   But maybe we could . . . keep in touch?

Help each other heal?

Help each other process what the hell happened . . . here

Pip   Yeah, I think that would be good. And can I start by saying, and forgive me if this is . . . but can I start by saying that I think you should probably leave this place?

Estella   Yeah, you're probably right, but where would I go?

Pip   I don't know! But I think it would be good for you.

Estella   Yup. I hear you on that.

And can *I* start by saying that I think *you* should probably go home?

Pip   You're probably right, but what would I do there?

Estella   I don't know but I think it would be good for you.

Pip   Yup. I hear you on that. Yup.

. . .

See you soon, Estella ?

Estella   See you soon, Pip.

Pip Returns to the Forge

Pip *arrives in the forge exactly as it was at the top of the show.*

He looks around the place taking it all in.

He takes off his hat and sets it down.

He takes off his jacket.

He sees there is a slight ember in the fire.

He pokes is cane in the ashes.

He rolls his sleeves up.

He pokes at it again.

Pip   OK. How do I?

Where do I?

He looks a moment longer at the embers.

OK. And that brings us to here.

Joe *enters, delighted to see* **Pip**.

Pip   Here we are.

We are here.

We are here.

And that's all that matters.

He looks round again, there's a hint of contentment and laughs a little to himself.

It's awrite this, aint it?

Joe   Aye, it is.

Pip   It's awrite this.

He begins in the process of making a nail.

The lights dim around him and the fire intensifies as he shapes out the side and he bangs harder and harder until, with brute force, he smashes down with a BANG.

End.

9 781350 456921